Thick Thighs, Tattoos & Breaking Taboos

Thick Thighs, Tattoos & Breaking Taboos

Jen Hoye

Cover design and interior layout by the author

For more information, visit https://www.jenniferhoye.com or contact healingmiles41@gmail.com

For Jimmy, Abby, and Joey

You are my heart, my greatest joy, and the reason I keep going, even on the hardest days. Never doubt that you are loved beyond measure.

And for Teddy

My brother, my first best friend, my forever pain in the ass. I would give anything to have you here, but since I can't, I'll keep saying your name, telling your stories, and making sure the world never forgets you. This book exists because of love and because of you.

"Jen Fusco Hoye tells it exactly like it is—with humor, heartbreak, and unflinching honesty. This book made me feel seen and heard in ways I didn't expect. One moment I was laughing out loud, the next I was in tears. It's not a self-help book, and it still helps—through raw truth, beautifully told stories, and the powerful reminder that we're not alone. Jen's voice is fierce, funny, deeply personal, and refreshingly unapologetic. This isn't just a book about grief—it's a rally cry for advocacy, connection, and breaking the silence around suicide loss."

~ Caro Brookings, suicide bereavement coach and author of *Hope: Rewiring Your Brain After Suicide Loss*

"Jen is running for her brother, Teddy, she is running for herself, and she is running for the communal, overwhelming agony of those who have lost loved ones to suicide just as she has, dedicating her last healing mile to each and every one of them. Along her path of advocacy, strangers become confidants of their shared pain.

Determined to transform the alchemy of her profound grief into action, Jen's perseverance rescued her from her doldrums. Her mission is to do the same for others in similar distress.

Her memoir is so engrossing, I felt I was running stride for stride beside her on every page. You will as well! Her powerful quest, step by step, word by word, and your journey as the reader of her book are both well worth taking."

~ Michael Cloherty, author of *Abel Bodied: Murder at the Malden Bank*

This book would not exist without the people who helped carry me through grief, through healing, and through every messy middle in between. (So. Much. Mess.)

To my children, Jimmy, Abby, and Joey: You are and will always be my "why." Thank you for loving me exactly as I am, even when I'm out "Deetzing" it up, embarrassing you with my laugh, and rage cleaning. You keep me grounded, humbled, and laughing. I am endlessly proud to be your mom.

To Teddy. Oh, Fuckin' Teddy. I miss you every day. I wish this weren't the story I had to write. But since it is, I'll keep telling it loudly and unapologetically, with love, laughter, rage, and reverence. This book is for you.

To my parents: I know this book is hard. Thank you for letting me tell the truth and trusting that it's told with love. I know it has not been easy for you or our family, and I love you. Thank you for telling me you are proud of me, even though I know I'm A LOT. You taught me to love fiercely, speak honestly, and never forget what matters. You always had my back, even when we didn't have the words. And, MG, thank you for being such a good sport about my menagerie of animals, naming all of my chickens after you, and letting me share your photo on the internet "for the whole town to see."

To James and both of our extended families: Thank you for always believing in me. I love you and appreciate you more than you could imagine.

To my sister-friends—Jenn, Kris, Vicki G., April, Vicki H., Guadalupe, Morgan, Laura, Jessica, Kerri and Meg AKA "Cool Bitches," Nichole, Erica May, Lila, Jessi, Amanda, Sarah A., Melissa, Sadie; Mario and Dave (you're not sister-friends, but you might as well be!); and so many more that I am sure that I am forgetting too many: Thank you for holding me up, handing me tissues and dirty martinis, sending memes, and reminding me who I am when I forget. Your presence in my life is sacred.

To the incredible beta readers who gave their time, their honesty, and their pens: Erica DeSimone Capogreco, Holly Herring, Adrienne Mattson, Ann Marie Mills, Heidi Ricker, Mike and Jen Cloherty, and Caro Brookings. THANK YOU for your honest feedback and reactions. You made this book sharper, braver, and better. A special thank you to authors Mike Cloherty (author of *Abel Bodied: Murder at the Malden*

Bank) and Caro Brookings (suicide bereavement coach and author of *Hope: Rewiring Your Brain After Suicide Loss*) for your feedback and kind words.

To my fellow survivors of suicide loss, of mental health battles, of life itself: You are not alone. Thank you for walking (and running) with me. I see you. I carry your stories with me across so many Healing Miles.

To all of the incredible organizations and every person I've met in this work: American Foundation for Suicide Prevention (AFSP), Samaritans, The Kacie Project (and founder Steve Palm), the Massachusetts Coalition for Suicide Prevention (and all their local chapters), Angie Comeford, Clinton Baker, The Surviving Siblings Podcast and Maya, Melissa from The Leftover Pieces, Dr. Angela Dean of The Broken Pack, and so many more: Thank you for giving me space to turn pain into purpose and connection. My life is forever changed because of the people I've met on this journey.

To nutrition and fitness coach Elena Green, thank you for building EG Fit and showing me that I *can* do hard things.

To the running community, especially my beautiful and unhinged band of Misfit Runners: Thank you for showing up on the good and hard days and being a fantastic example for me. For every finish line photo, every "you've got this" in the comments, and every juvenile meme and tussle story ever. Tiffany, Christianna, Carrie, Buck (and Shirley!), Lauren, Darren, Amy, Natalia, Shereen, Jesse, Lori, Brent, Phil, BD, founder Marcus, and so many more, you all get me and are still here for more. Hahahaha.

Finally, to the readers: Thank you for picking up this book. Whether you're here for the humor, the heartbreak, the healing, or all of it, thank you for sitting with me in the hard stuff. May you find your own truth in these pages. May you feel less alone.

Now go do something bold. Preferably with coffee.

LANGUAGE WARNING

If you are easily offended by swear words, turn back now.

CONTENT WARNING

This book contains discussions of suicide, grief, mental health struggles, and non-suicidal self-injury (NSSI). These topics are deeply personal and may be difficult for some readers.

While I approach them with honesty—sometimes raw, sometimes with humor, and always with love—I recognize that not everyone processes these subjects in the same way.

Please take care of your well-being while reading. It's okay to step away or skip sections. And it's always OK to reach out for help.

You are not alone.

If you or someone you love is struggling, help is available.

United States

- 988 Suicide & Crisis Lifeline – Dial 988 or visit 988lifeline.org (24/7, free, confidential support)
- Crisis Text Line – Text HELLO to 741741 (24/7 support)
- The Trevor Project (LGBTQ+ youth) – Call 1-866-488-7386, text START to 678678, or visit thetrevorproject.org
- Veterans Crisis Line – Dial 988, then press 1 or text 838255

Canada

- 988 Suicide & Crisis Lifeline – Dial 988 or visit 988.ca (24/7, free, confidential support)
- Talk Suicide Canada – Call 1-833-456-4566 or visit talksuicide.ca
- Hope for Wellness (Indigenous support) – Call 1-855-242-3310 or visit hopeforwellness.ca
- Trans Lifeline – Call 1-877-330-6366

United Kingdom

- Samaritans – Call 116 123 or visit samaritans.org
- Shout Crisis Text Line – Text SHOUT to 85258
- PAPYRUS HOPELINEUK (for people under 35) – Call 0800 068 4141, text 07860 039967, or visit papyrus-uk.org

Australia

- Lifeline Australia – Call 13 11 14 or visit lifeline.org.au
- Suicide Callback Service – Call 1300 659 467
- Kids Helpline – Call 1800 55 1800 (ages 5-25)

Other International Resources

- International Suicide Prevention Directory – findahelpline.com (global directory of crisis helplines)
- Befrienders Worldwide – befrienders.org (support services across multiple countries)

Please call your local emergency number if you are in immediate danger or need urgent help.

This isn't a 'How to Heal' book. It's a 'Holy Shit, Healing is Messy and Weird' book.

I never thought I'd author a book about grief, running, and mental health, but here we are. Because life is unpredictable and occasionally ridiculous ... Sometimes in all the best ways and sometimes in ways that tear you into a million jagged pieces.

If you had told me years ago that I'd lose my brother Teddy to suicide and find my path toward healing by pouring my heart out (on social media, no less) about losing my brother, battling my own mental health struggles, and somehow tying it all together with long runs and dark humor, I would've laughed in your face. I'd have balked if you'd told me I would be open with my thoughts or feelings alone. It wasn't who I was in the time BEFORE. And don't get me started on running ... I once thought about adding a "0.0" sticker to my car! (I write a lot about the time BEFORE and AFTER Teddy's death. The capitalization of the words is intentional, as many loss survivors can relate to.)

And yet, this book demanded to be written.

Because grief is relentless. Because mental health struggles don't just "go away." Because running saved me, except when it didn't. Because too many of us are walking around with stories we think we're supposed to keep quiet about because they make other people uncomfortable.

This book is my way of saying, fuck that.

*****

I lost my brother Teddy Fusco, Jr., to suicide on May 5, 2017.

That moment forever divided my life into the BEFORE and AFTER. While everything changed, the world kept spinning like it hadn't just shattered around me.

In the middle of trying to survive grief, I realized something: We are so bad at talking about loss and mental health. We whisper about it; we avoid it; we drown it in bullshit platitudes like "everything happens for a reason" (spoiler: it doesn't) and "time heals all wounds" (it doesn't do that, either).

For the first three years, I did not process the grief at all. I focused on being strong for my parents and kids and tried to return to "normal" life, not realizing that life no longer existed. I stuffed down my overwhelming feelings with food, alcohol, shopping, and self-harm. I barely slept, staying awake all night to watch reruns of *Law & Order: SVU*. I was filled with a white-hot rage that I took out on everyone, but mostly on myself.

Those first few years, I wasn't living. I was going through the motions and taking up space. My mental health was at its unhealthiest, and my physical health wasn't far behind. I'd gained nearly one hundred pounds, my stomach constantly felt like an acid pit, and I caught every virus, bug, and crud with which I came into contact.

In so many ways, it felt like I had died with Teddy. I didn't care because I felt like the universe got it wrong. Teddy was too good to be dead. It should have been me.

And then, the COVID-19 global pandemic struck. Everything shut down, and I found myself never alone. While I loved not obsessing over my kids' whereabouts, I hated that I was never alone in my house because all of my self-destructive coping skills—binge eating, shopping, drinking, self-harm—required secrecy.

I didn't want to sit in my pain forever, but I also didn't want to pretend it wasn't there, so I ran ... Literally.

However, not in the beginning. At first, I walked to the end of my street and back—seven hundred feet each way—and needed to take several breaks because I was that physically deconditioned.

While I panted and sweated the entire time, I also noticed something else: I felt slightly better emotionally. I won't lie. This release was partly due to the words I spoke aloud to my brother during this first walk: "Fuckin' Teddy."

Over time, the walks got longer, and my conversations with Teddy grew kinder. Though if you knew Teddy in his lifetime, you probably also knew that "Fuckin' Teddy" could be a term of frustration or endearment.

*****

Coincidence accounts for so many happenings in my life since Teddy died. Or serendipity. Or maybe just some cosmic Teddy prank.

Running was one of those things. I never planned on transitioning from walking to running, but it happened thanks to my brother Teddy. (More on that later.)

At first, I ran to escape the overwhelming sadness, guilt, and anger. Then, I ran because it gave me something to hold onto when everything else felt unsteady. I ran through grief, through depression, through the days I could barely get out of bed. Running didn't fix me, but it kept me moving.

And somewhere between mile markers and breakdowns, I realized that my healing wasn't supposed to look pretty. It was supposed to be messy, awkward, weird, and mine.

And I started sharing in the one way I'd always felt comfortable: through writing.

I've written and shared on social media each morning for several years. I write about suicide loss and grief, my brother, whatever I'm feeling or experiencing at the moment, or just a mental health topic that feels right.

Each post includes a photo of my morning coffee (in a mug most often "inappropriate") resting on my legs. Over the years, these legs have come to include beautiful artwork—colorful tattoos, each with deep significance and typically tied to a memorable moment. My sister-friend Sarah once referred to my morning reflections as the Leg Blog.

That's the book you're holding in your hands.

Well, mostly. I've assembled a selection of these Leg Blog posts, edited or expanded them, and made sense of the most implausible moments in my history. I hope my experience can help even one person feel less alone.

There are no five easy steps to healing or motivational quotes about finding joy. If you're looking for a polished, inspirational guide with a happy little bow tied around it, you're in the wrong frigging place.

But if you're looking for brutal honesty, dark humor, and a whole lot of swearing? Pull up a chair, my friend.

We don't talk enough about the hard shit. We tiptoe around grief and mental illness, like saying the words out loud will somehow make it worse. But silence doesn't save lives. Talking does.

This book is my way of telling the truth: the raw, unfiltered, sometimes hilarious, and occasionally heartbreaking truth about what it means to lose someone you love and somehow keep going.

I want this book to be what I needed when I was lost and drowning in grief—the one that says, "You're not crazy. You're not broken. You're human. And you loved deeply."

This book is part memoir, part rant about how society sucks at handling grief, and part love letter to my brother, running, advocacy, and tattoos that tell stories.

If you've ever felt like your pain was too much, your grief was too messy, or your healing wasn't happening fast enough, I see you.

May 7, 2017

It is with an incredibly heavy heart that I share the news that we lost my brother Teddy on Friday, May 5, 2017.

He was a beloved son, brother, grandson, nephew, cousin, friend, and everyone's favorite Uncle.

As many of you know, Teddy was born nearly four months early—a miracle in so many ways. He was called to Heaven decades too soon. My family and I feel lucky to have shared the 41 short years we had with Teddy.

Teddy was loved by all, and it's no surprise that he had so many who held him dear. I'm not saying this as his sister, but as someone who was amazed on a daily basis by his kindness, gentle soul, and genuine and unending capacity for love.

Teddy would give you the shirt off his back, even amid a blizzard and subzero temperatures. But, of course, only after he helped shovel out your car, made you his famous nuclear-hot chicken legs or barbecue ribs, and then cleaned your home until it was sparkling.

I see much of Teddy's sense of humor in Joey, which brings me joy. From a young age, Teddy loved to make everyone around him laugh. We have so many "Teddy stories" that it's difficult to pick a favorite. He was also a practical joker, encouraging Jimmy's April Fool's ideas and playing many jokes on friends, family, and colleagues.

Please keep our family in your prayers as we grieve the loss of this truly special angel. Teddy, I love you.

1

My Brother Teddy was a Pain in My Ass … And Life Without Him Sucks

One of my earliest memories is of going to "meet" Teddy after he was born. We were barely eighteen months apart, so I remember bits and pieces. It might not even be accurate, but the details I can recall are as vivid as if they just happened.

I was dressed in one of my best Polly Flinders dresses—light blue with yellow flowers, a wide lace yoke, and a tie in the back—with white tights and scuffed Mary Jane shoes. My hair had been brushed neatly by my Grandma Jennie, though pieces were already slipping out of the plastic daisy barrettes she'd fastened to keep the hair off my face.

I clearly remember being in the hospital elevator with Papa Joe, staying quiet because that was the rule. The elevator smelled funny, clean but also something else I didn't like, so I held my breath during the ride up, up, up. I charged ahead when the elevator doors opened, even though Papa told me to wait for him. I didn't care. I wanted to see my baby brother, Teddy.

That is all I remember, though the memory isn't as important as the emotions I felt as I pushed my way past the opening elevator doors: a swelling pride, love that bubbled up through my chest, and an intense feeling that I would protect my brother from anything and everything, always.

This memory presses on me many nights, crushing my chest and stopping my breath. Because I made a promise to my brother and broke it, I failed to protect Teddy when he needed it most.

*****

It is often said that grief is love with nowhere to go.

Some days, it hangs out on my shoulder, gently patting my back like a reassuring hand. Other times, it's a relentless, uninvited houseguest that refuses to leave.

Which is ironic. The last time Teddy came to my house for dinner (because we always remember the last moments) was in February 2017. He overstayed all our bedtimes. When he suggested we start watching a movie at 10 p.m., I told him the kids needed to get to sleep, and he needed to head home.

What I wouldn't give to have that opportunity back ... To do it right and ask him to sleep over and then join us for a pancake breakfast in the morning.

But I didn't. Instead, I spent most of the evening yelling at Teddy for riling up the kids, particularly six-year-old Joey, trying not to lose my shit, and begging them to calm the fuck down.

It's another in a long list of remembered moments I would alter if I could. I replay these moments on a loop, grasping for a version in which I was more patient, present, and attuned to the weight of time slipping through our fingers.

But Teddy is gone, leaving me with only a pile of photographs that will never grow, fading memories, and a laundry list of regrets.

*****

In September 2021, I had an opportunity to share my brother Teddy's life and my experience as a surviving sibling through an account takeover with the Surviving Our Siblings Instagram handle (@survivingoursiblings).

Much of this chapter contains modified content from that series because I believe it truly tells the story of my brother Teddy, our life together, and living and learning how to be and who to be without him.

I wrote in my introduction:

"... through the nearly forty-two years we had together. We were like one unit, 'Jennifer-and-Teddy' often felt like one name. One identity.

This fills me with the most terror of all the questions that often keep me awake into the early morning hours: Who am I without Teddy, and am I enough to fill the void he left behind?"

While even now, eight years after Teddy's death, I am still learning the answers to those questions, I am also discovering that although Teddy is not here physically, I carry him with me always.

*****

"My mama always told me that miracles happen every day. Some people don't think so, but they do." ~ Forrest Gump

Forrest Gump was one of Teddy's favorite movies. I think partly because he shared so many qualities with that lovable character: loyalty, honesty, integrity, kindness. Teddy would be there if you ever needed help, whether you asked for it or not. He'd be in the way, trying to make you smile with his jokes, and stay longer than you'd planned. But, he'd also make the situation better without even trying.

On more than one occasion, when I'd been rushed to the hospital, Teddy was the first to show up—no matter what time—so that I wouldn't be alone and scared. He never asked if I needed him there; he just showed up, because that's what he did. He was the one you could count on, no matter what.

Teddy wasn't just my brother; he was the keeper of small kindnesses. He noticed the little things—the way someone's coffee cup was almost empty, the way a jacket had slipped off the back of a chair, the way a person's shoulders tensed with stress—and he acted without hesitation.

He was the one who cleaned up after everyone without being asked. While we were still laughing, drinking, and eating at every family gathering, Teddy cleared plates, wiped counters, and ensured everything was in order.

Sometimes, Teddy didn't wait until you were finished, either. Many who knew him can recall when they were still eating and had a plate, cup, or whole place setting whisked away by "Fuckin' Teddy."

It used to frustrate me—and so many others–but in a smiling, head-shaking, "Fuckin' Teddy," endearment kind of way. I wondered why he couldn't just sit and enjoy the moment.

But now, I realize that was his way of showing love. It was who he was. But, I'm getting ahead of myself. Let me start at the beginning.

*****

My brother Teddy was born in 1975, nearly four months early, weighing just half a pound—small enough to fit in the palm of a hand. A fragile, impossible thing. His twin, Joseph, survived only a few hours, and Teddy remained in the NICU at Boston Children's Hospital for months, fighting for every breath.

Our big Sicilian family did what they did best ... They prayed. My great-grandmother, whom we all called "Big Grandma," led the charge, calling on the intercession of Saint Agrippina di Mineo. Alongside her, fellow Boston Saint Agrippina Society members lifted their voices, believing faith and sheer will could tip the scales in Teddy's favor.

For those unfamiliar with Saint Agrippina, she was a beautiful blonde princess who was brutally tortured and martyred in AD 256, under Emperor Valerian. After her death, three devout women smuggled her body from Rome to Mineo, Sicily, on a treacherous journey filled with miracles. A divine cloud shielded them from pursuers, and angels protected them from harm, ensuring Agrippina's remains would find sanctuary.

Teddy's survival felt like a miracle of its own. A boy who was never meant to live defied the odds at every turn. And when he finally came home from the hospital, he was celebrated—not just by our family but by Boston's entire North End—at the annual Feast of St. Agrippina. The prayers had worked. He had made it.

Teddy was always special, a miracle in every way, making losing him much more unbearable.

*****

Teddy loved to make people laugh with jokes, impressions, and most definitely pranks. The more outlandish, the better.

Sometimes, he did things just because he was impulsive and curious. And those things typically became a "Teddy Story," told forever and always ending with a shake of the head, a chuckle, and "Fuckin' Teddy."

When he was small—maybe four or five—Teddy sprayed our neighbors, the Spencers, with the garden hose to see what might happen. They were headed to a party, possibly a wedding, dressed in their nicest party clothes. From inside the house, we heard the screams of "TEDDY, NOOOO!" While Teddy was most definitely grounded as a result, it was one of those uniquely Teddy stories that we often recalled and always laughed about.

He always encouraged my son Jimmy's April Fool's Day pranks. Together, they replaced every photo of me in my house with a photocopied picture of Teddy. It took me hours to notice, but once I did, I kept finding more. It took me hours to remove them all.

Teddy once mailed a colleague a bologna sandwich in response to the man's daily comment, "Wow, I haven't had a bologna sandwich in years."

Even from beyond the grave, Teddy continued his jokes ...

Around one of Teddy's heavenly birthdays, I lovingly made a ham and cheese sandwich on white bread with mayonnaise. I packed it in a plastic sandwich bag, placed it in a padded envelope along with a pretty napkin, and mailed it to my cousin Michael.

I didn't realize until after I dropped the package into the mailbox that Michael had gone to Cape Cod for the week with his sons to escape the record heat of that July. When Michael returned home from vacation, he said he could smell the package before opening it. Although his three young sons encouraged him to eat the sandwich, Michael could not take even one bite for fear of food poisoning.

Several years back, my kids (Jimmy, Abby, and Joey) thought up a prank to scare me. And, rather than jump out from somewhere, which would have been more than adequate, they Teddy-leveled it. I'd just returned from a walk, and Joey popped up from under the kitchen island in an obvious way. I wasn't too scared and told him to stop so I could get dinner started. While I was talking to Joey and Abby, Jimmy popped out of the closet and shouted, "BOO!" Abby, for her part, giggled her cute little giggle while the boys congratulated one another on their master plan. I stood there with wet pants because I had quite literally pissed myself ... It's something I would've called Teddy to share, to hear him giggle like Abby; but once I reached for my phone, reality felt oh so heavy.

*****

In most of our childhood photos, I've my arm protectively around Teddy, even though it might have looked like a headlock.

While I relished informing him anytime he broke the "rules," which was often, my implied role as Teddy's protector trumped all.

Teddy was a sweet boy with an impish sense of humor and a golden heart that matched his angelic blonde curls. Many kids took advantage of his kind nature and teased him about his small size or his big ears. I thought his ears were adorable, but kids and adults alike latched onto this feature, often calling Teddy "Dumbo."

I was perpetually disheveled and had perfected my RBF (resting bitch face) during infancy it seems. I was also ready to fight anyone who bothered my brother (even kids years older and much larger than I). Kids who called him terrible, hurtful names, took his lunchbox (or his lunch), and tied him to a stop sign and lit firecrackers at his feet. Anything at all. I was ready to go.

Pretty soon, kids at school knew: "Don't mess with Teddy Fusco because his sister will kick your ass."

Of course, Teddy always tried to persuade me to handle things more calmly. We never told our parents any of this for fear that he'd be punished for not standing up for himself and I'd be punished for fighting (so unladylike!).

Still, when Teddy was born, I promised to protect him always. Yet, in the biggest fight of his life, I failed. This will always haunt me.

Although Teddy and I only had one another as siblings, we grew up part of a large Sicilian family. Mom is one of four daughters, and my grandparents' siblings and their kids and grandkids were all considered just "family." Not first cousins, twice removed, but family.

A traditional Sicilian-American family meant Sunday dinners, big holidays—birthdays, anniversaries, Saint days, and more—and "family first." There was never a shortage of food, laughter, or cousins to play with.

Our grandparents, Jennie and Joe, were the center of our universe—and everyone else's. Most of my happiest memories occurred at their home in Chelsea, Massachusetts.

Papa Joe passed away in 2011, fracturing Mom's family and marking the beginning of Grandma Jennie's decline. Teddy, unmarried and childless, made sure to stop by their house often, shoveling, doing yard work, and listening to their stories. After Papa died, Teddy's visits increased, something Grandma Jennie loved and appreciated.

Grandma's death in December 2016 was devastating for my entire family, including both Teddy and me, even though she was 92. She was our family's matriarch, the one who loved us fiercely and always had our backs. Grandma Jennie was the one truly consistently safe person in our lives.

I now recognize that Grandma's passing was just one of what is called a "triggering factor" in relation to my brother's death by suicide. I often think I should have done more to support Teddy during that time ... That's what is known in the suicide loss survivor community as the "tyranny of hindsight," and it's yet another thing that fills me with guilt.

*****

Teddy was a Department of Conservation and Recreation Ranger at the Massachusetts State House for nearly twenty years. He loved Boston; his photo albums are filled with photos he'd captured around the city over the years. Today, Teddy's photo albums are among my most treasured possessions.

During his tenure, Teddy was known for being kind, helpful, and a devious prankster. Rangers have shared tales of some of his jokes, and I even wonder how he could be so creative.

His friend and fellow Ranger, Debbie, died in April 2017, just one month before Teddy, following a decades-long battle with cancer. They shared common interests and supported one another through many challenges. While their relationship was not romantic, I honestly believe they were soulmates.

Local media forever captured Teddy and Debbie in two iconic photos. One shows them walking through Boston's Columbus Park at Christmastime; in the other, they're doing the infamous ALS Ice Bucket Challenge on the steps of the Massachusetts State House, both laughing.

This photo is often used in online articles and news segments related to the ALS charity challenge, and even once on a Today Show segment on viral fundraising. When it appears, I feel shocked, holding my breath and trying to hear his giggle until the image is gone. I rewind the TV over and over, hoping to catch something, anything that could have hinted at what was to come.

Because I never saw it coming. None of us did.

*****

The week that Teddy died, he had been trying to talk some sense into me before I brought home six baby chicks without asking my husband, James. Of course, I didn't listen, and days before my twentieth wedding anniversary, I showed up with chickens that James didn't want. James was so angry that he didn't speak to me for days, and I was not handling being on the receiving end of the silent treatment well.

Teddy texted me daily memes and jokes to try to cheer me up. On James's and my anniversary, Teddy sent me a GIF of Homer Simpson walking down a flight of stairs in a wedding gown and asked if that's how James had dressed that morning for work, which couldn't be further from James's typical attire of a white shirt, dark pants, and quiet tie.

That weekend, I was scheduled to fly to Las Vegas for work. I hadn't texted with Teddy in a few days but didn't think much of it. I was stressed out, wrapped up in the chicken drama, Abby's community play performance, and preparing for a busy workweek in Las Vegas.

Like most, I will never forget the moment that I heard that we lost Teddy. I listened to the agony in my parents' voices and cries. Of calling Jimmy to come home immediately, then explaining to the kids that Uncle Teddy had gone to heaven. While we'd told Jimmy and Abby that evening, we waited until six-year-old Joey woke up. For nearly one year, Joey had difficulty sleeping because he worried that if he fell asleep, someone would be dead when he woke up.

Teddy was just forty-one years old. This was not supposed to happen.

*****

It's taken me years to verbalize this. Still, I remember the day after Teddy died with a searing anger and resentment. I've often felt robbed of a significant time alone with my parents as we first started to process Teddy's suicide. In retrospect, I understand that those feelings are misplaced, instead representative of me looking for anyone to blame for this tragedy. Now I feel grateful for my large extended family, whose love and support buoyed us through the initial shock and disbelief, long after others had faded into their everyday activities and lives. Talk about the tyranny of hindsight.

I live about an hour south of Boston and the surrounding cities, where most of my family still lives. I'd wanted to drive up to my parents' house on the night of May 5, but we agreed I'd wait until the morning.

After a sleepless night, James, the kids, and I piled into the car to drive to my parents' house. I have no memory of that trip, save for the feeling of disbelief ... This couldn't be true. Teddy was not dead. This was not happening. Suicide happens to other families. Not ours.

Yet, I knew. Teddy was gone; he had taken his own life. Nothing would ever be the same. The closer we got to my parents, the heavier this reality felt.

(I will not detail my parents' state that morning. They've lived through the worst possible pain any parent could survive, and those first moments with them will remain forever private. You'll learn that while I am open with my experience as a suicide loss survivor, there are just some things that I choose to hold in my heart. This is one of them. If you have lost someone to suicide, I imagine that you too understand this need to contain specific details and moments that are simply too painful and activating.)

Before we sat down to comfort one another, and before I even had a chance to hug my parents long and hard, I heard a quick knock at the door. My Auntie Jean, one of Mom's three sisters, and her daughter, Stephanie, had arrived to offer comfort and share our profound disbelief and excruciating sorrow. The rest of our family followed them: Auntie Judy, Auntie Ann, Uncle Buddy, cousins Michael and Nicole, and Nicole's daughters, Mia and Katie.

It was a full house. We sat crammed into my parents' open living and dining rooms. It felt almost like a holiday, but without the laughter and noise—like a holiday, but with one person conspicuously and painfully missing.

The room remained silent for a bit, each of us lost in our own grief, every few moments punctuated by a muffled sob. My head was spinning, my eyes throbbing from crying all night. I couldn't think straight and heard a buzzing sound in my ears. No, a whirring, more like a low-pitched hum.

Whir, hum, stop.
Whir, hum, stop.
Whir, hum, stop.

The noise stopped and started again. Was I imagining it? Turning my head toward the sound, I realized my young cousin was twirling a fidget spinner over and over.

Whir, hum, stop.
Whir, hum, stop.
Whir, hum, stop.

A white hot rage bubbled up inside me. My body felt hot, burning from the inside out, and I fought to remain seated. Although my cousin was just a child who was coping with a tragedy in the best way possible for her, I imagined violently ripping that fidget spinner from her hands and hurling it over my parents' balcony into the ocean with a loud "Fuck you!" directed at no one and everyone.

Whir, hum, stop.

Whir, hum, stop.

Whir, hum, stop.

Whir, hum, stop.

Whir, hum, stop.

Whir, hum, stop.

And yet, Teddy remained dead. Gone forever.

*****

I do not recall the exact specifics, but I insisted on accompanying my father to Teddy's East Boston condo to get a suit for the burial. My parents tried to talk me out of going to protect me, but that stubborn streak won out, and I went with Dad.

Although my brother had lived in his condo for some time, it was only the second time I'd ever been inside. This wasn't unusual, because we generally got together every Sunday at our grandparents' house and (after their passing) at Mom and Dad's or Auntie Jean's homes. There just hadn't been a reason to make a separate trip.

Contrary to what happens in the movies, Teddy had not left a note. Today, I recognize that this is often the case, and many families spend days, years, even decades trying to answer that one crushing question, "Why?"

But that day, when I walked into Teddy's tidy condo, I was on a mission. I wanted to uncover the truth behind this final decision. There had to be an explanation, and I would find it. My logical and orderly mind would not accept any other option.

To call Teddy's place "tidy" is more of an understatement than anything. His condo was pristine. Not a speck of dust. Not a single thing out of place. Even the magnets on the fridge were perfectly aligned.

I've always considered myself a neat freak, but Teddy took it to another level. When he still lived at home, Dad often put his coffee cup down on the counter, walked away to do something, and then returned to find it washed and returned to the cupboard. Each year in July, Teddy and his friends rented a house in New Hampshire. His friends Tracy and Kerri could always count on Teddy to clean up after dinner, even if they weren't finished. They told me that Teddy scrubbed a baking sheet and restored it to its original luster, which Kerri had attempted for months without success.

That other time I'd visited Teddy's condo, I secretly tipped a few photos hanging on the wall to be a jerk. Teddy never mentioned finding his gallery wall askew. Still, I imagine him muttering swearwords while he restored the photographs to their original, perfect alignment.

This day was no different—everything was exactly as it should be, as if Teddy had just stepped out to run an errand. Yet, his absence hung heavy in the darkened rooms. I ran my hand along the top of a bookcase filled with photo albums ... All of Teddy's captured memories stored in perfect chronological order. I wondered what he was thinking in those final moments.

I got to work, looking for a note, a clue, a reason ... Something; anything to help me make even a little sense of this waking nightmare.

Starting in Teddy's second bedroom, which he used as an office, I looked through and under every drawer, flipping through notebooks to see if I could make out the press of a pen on any of the blank pages. Nothing.

I spotted a cigar box in the living room—something Teddy had long used to hold mementos. Inside, I found his one-year chip from Alcoholics Anonymous, a card from the people at his regular meeting celebrating his sobriety achievement, random trinkets, and ticket stubs from sports games and Chris Stapleton concerts.

There were cards along the windowsill behind his couch, expressing sympathy for the loss of his dear friend Debbie, who lost her long battle with cancer only weeks before. Sympathy cards stacked in the corner, from just several months prior, just after our Grandma Jennie passed. There were several of them from 2011, when Papa Joe died. Each of these deaths had deeply affected Teddy, but was that enough for this?

I went through every photo album, nearly twenty in total. Photography was one of Teddy's many creative hobbies. His albums contained photos from every party, every get-together, every holiday, every vacation. Visits to Revere Beach during the annual sandcastle competition. Beautiful perspectives of the Massachusetts State House taken from all angles, likely during or after his shift as a Ranger with the Massachusetts Department of Conservation and Recreation. And my kids, Jimmy, Abby, and Joey. So many photos of my kids throughout their lives, enjoying time with their Uncle Teddy.

One album surprised me. Instead of photographs, it contained prayer cards for possibly every single wake or funeral Teddy had attended in his lifetime. The final one was of someone who'd only just recently passed away, and whose services were only a few days earlier. I didn't recognize the person, but she must have mattered enough for Teddy to save her prayer card. I asked Dad, who said Teddy had taken the day off from work to attend the wake and funeral. I wondered if this death had reminded Teddy of Debbie, Grandma Jennie, and Papa Joe? Was it a catalyst?

I don't know what I expected to find in Teddy's pantry, but I went through that, too. All I found, though, was an ideally stored supply of pasta, canned and dry goods, toilet paper, and paper towels. We'd learned from Grandma Jennie to buy these things when they were on sale and store them, so we'd never run out even if something happened. We didn't ever know what that "something" could be, but I imagine this was a legacy of growing up during the Great Depression.

Next, Teddy's bedroom, where he'd spent his final moments. Where Dad found his son's lifeless body, the paramedics found the gun and quickly moved my father out of the room, where crime scene cleaners had removed evidence of what happened.

I didn't get this far to stop here. I crossed the threshold, holding my breath, half expecting to feel a jolt or a chill as I entered … But this was not a movie. It was real life, and all I felt was a crushing pain in my chest and wet tears spilling from my eyes.

Again, I searched every drawer, pulling them out and checking the undersides. Nothing. Pulled the dresser away from the wall—a large manila envelope. I called for Dad. As I unfastened the clasp and pulled out the sheets of paper inside, I held my breath.

"Are you fucking kidding me?" I yelled. This was not what I expected. It was a recipe. A fucking recipe.

"Polish Hunter's Stew. The most disgusting thing Teddy ever made. And he was so proud of it," Dad said.

Talk about a "Fuckin' Teddy" moment.

There had to be something.

Some clue.

Some reason.

Something.

Anything.

Maybe the closet? Yet, that was another dead end. Teddy's clothes, organized by work, casual, and in color order, hung perfectly in his neat closet. No hidden box on the shelf. Nothing in the neat line of shoes.

But a backpack. Unzipping the front pocket, I pulled out several energy bars. Confused, I continued examining the contents, realizing that although it was only May, Teddy was already packed for his annual July camping trip with friends. We'd talked about it the week before. Teddy looked forward to this trip every year, which always fell during his birthday week. I thought of his friends, who would be taking this trip without Teddy and his antics, and cried quietly with my hand on the wall.

The crime scene cleaners had missed a spot below where my hand rested. This is another one of those things that I will not detail, though it is the source of many nightmares and regular flashbacks. Probably the one thing that my parents wanted to protect me from when they tried to talk me out of going to Teddy's condo. What I write next is that I have never told another soul.

A piece of my brother was left behind. I wanted to keep it forever, but short of cutting out the drywall, which wasn't possible. I still regret not figuring out how to bring Teddy home with me.

*****

While I shouldn't have been surprised, I remember how overwhelmed I felt when I looked up from the car at the cemetery to see hundreds of people waiting at the graveside service—people whose lives my brother Teddy touched in one way or another. I will never forget their kindness, support, and compassion.

But, as many in our club will tell you, suicide loss is isolating. At home. At work. Even in a crowded auditorium. I felt alone. Other. Empty. And then angry. Filled with blinding rage. How could Teddy have chosen this?

Teddy abandoned me. I knew I would never be enough to fill the void he left behind. He was the good one; he should be here. Not me.

I didn't feel like I deserved to be alive.

And so I sank. Deeper and deeper in a life of despair, insomnia, binge eating, shopping, and television watching. I was alive but not living.

*****

I know that the impact that my brother's suicide has had on my kids, Jimmy, Abby, and Joey, is profound and compounded by the "loss" of their mother during a time when they desperately needed me. I will never forgive myself for abandoning the promise I made to myself when I became a mother: To always be present for my kids, support their difficult emotions, and show them that they are loved more than life itself. I regret the years spent in the fog of hopelessness and despair that I can never get back, never fix for my three hearts that beat outside my body. I will work to make this up to them for the rest of my days.

*****

I recently binge-watched a series where one of the main characters tells another, "You don't have the luxury of grief... People are counting on you." (From the MGM series *From*, 2023)

That line took me back to the days right after Teddy's death. People kept telling me to stay strong for my parents, kids, work, and normalcy. But what does "strong" even mean when your entire world has imploded?

I remember that first Christmas. My parents were in Florida, and I was home alone on Christmas Eve because the kids needed routine. I couldn't bear the thought of celebrating with nearly one hundred relatives (not an exaggeration, either). Instead, I sat in an empty house, grief suffocating me, turning everything black.

Grief had teeth. No, fangs, like the monsters in the series From. Razor-sharp and unforgiving, ripping me apart from the inside out.

Out of nowhere, my friend Mario texted. He was just checking in. He'd lost his father not long before, and somehow, he knew. He knew I was spiraling and needed someone to pull me back to the surface. That small moment of kindness—one text, one reminder that I wasn't alone—made all the difference. *(And yes, Mario, if you're reading this, you're still ugly and still a chooch.)*

Navigating the holiday season while grieving can be unbearable. If you're in it right now, please know you don't have to do it alone. And if you need someone to hear you, I'm here.

Grief has a way of making you feel like you should carry it alone. But I've learned that you do not have to be strong for anyone. You do not have to pretend. You do not have to hold it all inside. Feel your feelings, even the ugliest ones. Share them. Lean on those who love you. And when you see someone else drowning in their grief, be like Teddy: show up, stay longer than planned, and remind them they are not alone.

*****

"The Loss of History: Each family has its special history and the shared bonds that are a part of that history. When a sibling dies, the bonds are shattered, and history forever has a void that cannot be filled." (The Compassionate Friends. *Adults Grieving the Death of a Sibling.* https://www.compassionatefriends.org/adults-grieving-death-sibling/.)

I've struggled to tell our story without this part. Without Teddy, my history seems invalid some days.

I want to remain neutral, but like most families, our childhood wasn't always sunshine and roses. It was amazing and fun and all the things you'd expect growing up as a part of Gen X. Still, I recognize that our parents did the best they could with the tools they had. Mom was "mild" compared to Grandma Jennie in her heyday, and Dad grew up with significant trauma.

The weight of expectations pressed on each of us. Teddy, always "special" and smaller than most, usually in trouble, and not a great student. And me, a rule follower who aimed to keep everyone happy (or at least not angry) by helping without being asked, who never argued or talked back, and who always brought home straight As. Now I realize that we both felt like we would never be good enough, even though that was never our family's intention.

Sometimes, things were too quiet. Holidays especially. That's when we started hanging out in the back of my closet, sitting side-by-side on my Strawberry Shortcake sleeping bag underneath the rack of clothes and winter coats. Teddy drawing pictures or playing with Matchbox cars while I read with help from a little desk lamp connected to an extension cord. Both were snacking on full-sized candy bars that Grandma

Jennie snuck in brown paper bags, telling stupid jokes to make each other laugh.

Teddy, you were always enough.

2

Grief is Weird, and So Am I
(A Collection of Letters to My Brother)

That grief exists in stages is complete bullshit.

Denial.
Anger.
Bargaining.
Depression.
Acceptance.

When Elisabeth Kübler-Ross wrote *On Death and Dying* in 1969, I'm guessing that she didn't intend for readers to assume they'd move through the stages of grief in an orderly fashion, like ticking boxes on a checklist. But here we are, more than fifty years later, clinging to the idea that grief is a linear process with a clear beginning, middle, and end.

Grief is not linear. It's complicated and often messy. There are no rules. There is no map to the other side because "the other side" doesn't exist. There's no off-ramp from this horrible highway—grief becomes the road you travel, the backdrop of your life, sometimes a dull hum in the distance, sometimes a scream that drowns out everything else.

Some days, I think I'm learning that elusive acceptance piece—what it means to live as a sister without her brother. Other days, I find myself right back in the middle of a depressive episode or snapping with anger over the most minor things. And then, there are the days when I experience all five stages at once, like a chaotic, heavy-pour grief cocktail I never ordered.

I'm learning and relearning what grief means to me every single day, even years after my brother's death. Grief doesn't care about timelines or milestones; it shows up whenever it damn well pleases. It hides in the supermarket's aisles, lurking in the background music, ready to strike when a song you didn't even know meant anything suddenly becomes unbearable. It's in the quiet moments when you reach for your phone to text someone who isn't there anymore. It's in the laughter that feels too big for your chest, at a joke they would've loved, followed by tears because you can't share it with them.

When considered linearly, Kübler-Ross's stages suggest a final destination, a place where grief no longer rules your life. But that's not reality. For many of us, grief becomes a part of who we are; it's a shadow we carry with us, its weight shifting day by day. Sometimes it's light, almost unnoticeable. Other times, it's crushing, like a boulder on your chest.

I've accepted this, though I haven't entirely made peace with it. And maybe I never will. Grief, and that love with no place to go, still and will forever linger, heavy and unspent for the rest of my days.

Grief doesn't follow rules or always fit into neat, progressive stages, and that's okay. Life will never be the same. You will never be the same. Yet, through the pain, it's possible to live a life of beauty and meaning—a life filled with moments of joy and hope, even if they're tangled up with deep sorrow, anger, or emptiness.

Grief is absurd and disorganized, but it's also deeply human. If you're in it, you're not alone.

*****

I write a lot of letters to my brother in my posts. He'll never see them, but getting the words out into the world helps me. I feel that by sharing them, I can help others who are struggling with grief know that they are not alone, and that it's okay to talk to someone who's gone. These letters are my way of keeping Teddy's memory alive, saying the things I didn't get to say, and making sense of the mess that grief leaves behind. Maybe, in reading them, someone else will find a little piece of healing, too.

I didn't write or post letters to Teddy in 2018 or 2019 because I had deactivated my Facebook account. If you know me personally, you know how important social media has become in my healing journey.

The fact that I went "dark" during those years says more about my mental state than I can fully put into words. I wasn't processing anything—I was surviving. Looking back, it seems that I had been trapped in a fog, too overwhelmed to face the grief head-on, too broken to reach out.

Not writing to Teddy, not sharing those feelings, was like cutting off a lifeline I didn't even realize I needed.

*****

May 5, 2020

Teddy, it's been three years since you left us … 1,096 sunsets that you didn't see; Mother's and Father's Days, birthdays, and Christmases that your absence has marked; milestones for my kids that felt wrong without your presence and mischief. People say it gets easier, but people are wrong. I wake up every day hoping it was just a bad dream, that I'll receive a text about an open-faced turkey sandwich, or a funny card addressed to Nej; every night, I listen to the last voicemail you left me.

*****

For Teddy's anniversary on May 5, 2021, I walked in our hometown of Everett, Massachusetts. The following is a selection of my posts from that day. Ironically, my mileage that May coincided with Mental Health Awareness Month. It was part of an AFSP fundraiser called "Marathon in a Month," during which I pledged to walk three hundred miles in Teddy's and others' memories.

*****

May 5, 2021, 12:00 a.m.
Team AFSP Marathon in a Month, Day 17

I'll be walking later this morning, targeting twelve miles.

Right now, I can't sleep. Today is a bad day when nothing will ever be the same. Not our family. Not myself. Not the world. Things seem a little colder, darker, and less kind without Teddy.

And yet ... I see his smile and impulsivity in Joey. I hear his laugh in sweet Abby's giggle—his goddaughter carrying his tender heart. And his empathy and penchant for pranks and mischief are in Jimmy.

When Gus poops in the house, in my mind, I hear him calling the dog dis-GUS-ting and laughing like an idiot. When James reads his TV Guide, I think about Teddy's repeated offer to buy James a walker or other assistive device one might need when they're (ahem) much advanced in age. When I see Grape Nuts cereal in the supermarket, I remember the time he got them stuck to the ceiling, and they fell onto Mom's head.

And today, I feel his kindness everywhere. Your love and support have made this dark season bearable. For the first time in four years, I feel something different ...

Today, I feel hope.

*****

May 5, 2021, 6:03 a.m.

Care packages were made to share a message of hope and a cup of coffee with our hometown in memory of my brother Teddy.

I would give anything to share another meal with him. If you or someone you love is struggling, support and help are available.

*****

May 5, 2021, 9:44 a.m.

Hundreds of family members, friends, colleagues, and acquaintances attended Teddy's graveside service, effectively shutting down part of the city of Everett in the process. My early morning plans changed, so I started at your grave in Woodlawn Cemetery, and walked down Elm Street (with a stop to buy the M&M cookie I often spent my allowance on), past our elementary school, and then up Maplewood Avenue to our old house on Mt. Washington Street.

The neighborhood has changed, but I can still hear us yelling, playing kickball, and hide-and-seek with the hordes of neighborhood kids. Growing up in the free-range 1980s, our neighborhood crowd ran the street, only moving out of the way when someone yelled, "CAR!"

*****

May 5, 2021, 3:39 p.m.

A lot has changed in Everett, Massachusetts, since Teddy and I last lived there, but I'll always be an Everett Girl at heart.

Everett Mayor Carlo DeMaria, who grew up on "hospital hill" like us, was kind enough to meet with me this morning. We met outside the city's weekly food pantry, where Mayor DeMaria spoke with residents and volunteers. Despite the drizzly weather and his dress shoes, he offered to walk and talk with me about my "why," my purpose, and the significance of today.

I'm impressed with the city's commitment to youth mental well-being and offering social-emotional support to students, educators, and families. We walked nearly three miles together, bringing my total walking distance in Everett to almost six and a half miles. Like me, Mayor DeMaria is an avid walker, covering nearly seven miles daily!

On my walk through the city, I shared the care packages I had made to convey a message of hope and a cup of coffee in memory of my brother, Teddy. I met many kind people along the way. While I walked alone, I was never lonely.

After a nice lunch, I dropped my parents back at their condo and had a surprise meet-up (and a big hug) from my best friend, Jenn. I texted several of Teddy's closest friends. A dear friend asked her Pastor to say a special prayer for our family, and Nana had a mass said in Teddy's memory. All of your love and support helped us through this painful anniversary.

It'll never be the same, and Teddy's absence is something that we carry wherever we go. But I know he's walking beside me across every healing mile.

My heart is sad but at peace.

*****

July 10, 2021

Happy birthday in Heaven, Teddy. At [your best friend] John's suggestion, I thought of pranking someone in your honor today. I can still hear you laughing in my mind. I miss you and love you. Look out for us and Mom and Dad.

I brought ten Dunkin cards with me today in honor of Teddy's birthday but didn't see one person during my first two and a half miles. I guess five o'clock is not a popular hour on a Saturday morning. Who knew? (Teddy would've been awake, as we were both always early birds!)

Finally, I saw some people and mustered the courage to say, "Good morning. Today is my brother's birthday, and I'd like to share a cup of coffee with you in his memory" to the ten gift card recipients. Teddy would've liked it better if I'd awkwardly shoved the cards at them and shuffled away, but I wanted the world to know that Teddy is loved. I even got a hug from two people, which I was surprised I needed today.

I'm sending love to our family, Teddy's friends, and State House Ranger colleagues today. I feel loved and supported by so many. Thank you for checking on me.

Fellow sibling suicide loss survivor Samantha Seigler published a blog, and it captures perfectly everything about losing a sibling to suicide. Samantha is just one of the many bereaved siblings I've met along this grief journey, and while I'd much rather not have a reason to know them, each has touched my life most beautifully.

Thank you for putting them in my path, asshole.

*****

May 5, 2022

Teddy, how is it possible that you've been gone for five years?

We all miss you more than you could ever imagine. I try to be good to Ma and Dad, but I don't always get it right. I don't know how to help most days.

I see your gentle heart in Abby. Joey was cut from the same mold as you, and I love it, even when he drives me up a wall. And, as Jimmy gets older, he reminds me so much of you—sometimes, when he's watching a show, I hear him laugh and think it's you.

I feel you are with me, and I know you've put people on my path for a reason. While it comforts me, it would be better if you were here.

Most days, I can't help but think of you and mutter the line everyone knew well when you were alive: "Fuckin' Teddy." Some days, it makes me smile; others, I feel sadness, and others, I'm just angry.

Last night, I dreamed of two cardinals, whom I knew were Grandma Jennie and Papa Joe. As they walked toward me, a blue Jay swooped in again and again - I knew that was you, you giant pain in the ass. And then my phone rang. It was Auntie Marie telling me that you are all okay, we should lean on each other, and all of you are still with us all the time. That was the most beautiful dream ever.

*****

May 5, 2023

Teddy,

Ugh. Six years. Six whole years since any of us heard you laugh out loud or muttered, "Fuckin' Teddy." We all miss you so much. I try to do what I think you would for Ma and Dad, but even that doesn't always feel right.

You've missed so much again this year!

Jimmy has a "big boy job" and plays rugby. I know you would have supported his mission to see an otter while he was on a work trip on a research boat in Seattle. And you would LOVE his men's rugby team velour tracksuit. I can almost hear the 1980s Revere Beach references and jokes now.

Abby lives in Newport and has had a great school year. You would be so proud of her—she is conscientious and loves her first classroom experiences. Abby just performed with her dance team at school, which was beautiful.

Joey is more like you every single day. He's a total clown like you were and a rule follower like his mother, and he has Ma's smarts. Talk about a scary combination. He's still singing "Baby Got Back" all day, every day. Thanks for teaching it to him when he was three years old.

I'm still trying to run. I'll run my miles for you if I ever leave the house today. Yes, I'm slow. Yes, I've tripped. Yes, I've peed myself. And, yes, I've heard you laughing in my mind. But, you know, I won't give up, and for every single race, I save the last mile for you. I'm running a half marathon called the Cranky Crab this weekend, and the whole thing is for you.

*****

May 5, 2024

Teddy,

How have you been gone for seven years? Sometimes, I'm not sure—it feels like just yesterday.

Do you hear me talking to you? All. The. Damn. Time. You probably want me to shut up. But the joke's on you, I guess.

We all miss you. Your laugh. Your heart. Your foolishness. Saying, "Fuckin' Teddy."

I try hard to be good and do what you would for Ma and Dad. I know I don't always get it right, but I'm trying and always thinking, "What would Teddy do?"

You missed so much this year!

Jimmy bought his first home. Joey says, "Homeowner Jimmy is way less fun than regular Jimmy." He also celebrated two years of sobriety—I know you would be so proud of him.

Abby is getting ready to graduate from college! Can you believe it? She's had a fun senior year in Newport, and we saw her final performances with the Salve Regina University Dance Club. I know you would have been there cheering for her.

Joey is taller than I now, has a deep voice, and has sprouted a mustache. He started playing rugby like Jimmy, and he seems to really like it! I know you'd love to go to his games and watch him in action. He's so much like you that it sometimes takes my breath away.

I'm still running slowly. Do you hear every step I take? (Remember when you used to yell, "Boom Babba Boom" when I ran?) In the last year, I've brought you to many races in many places—including South Carolina and Virginia! I completed my first ultramarathon with forty frigging miles to celebrate my fiftieth birthday.

Yeah. I turned fifty, and you're forever frozen at forty-one. I don't like that this gap is growing.

I still feel you with me always, and I know you've put people in my path for a reason. This journey with the extended AFSP community has been so powerful. While it brings me comfort, it would be better if you were here.

Love you, jerk.

*****

July 10, 2024

Happy forty-ninth birthday in heaven, Teddy. Except you're not forty-nine. You're forty-one. Forever.

Each year, that age gap continues to widen. And, with it, the sadness of your absence. People who say "time heals all wounds" haven't experienced loss, in my opinion.

I remember growing up, I couldn't stand how close we were in age. It meant we had to do everything together, and I had to be the "responsible" one. Whenever I complained, Mom would say, "Someday, all you'll have is each other." And I'd always storm off, pissed that I was forced to include you.

What I wouldn't give to have you here still. To beg you to stop getting Joey riled up. I want to tell you and Abby to stop giggling at family events. To call you and Jimmy "jerks" for getting me yet again with one of your jokes. To navigate this adult life together, all of the ups and downs and in-betweens.

On your anniversary (or angelversary as I like to call it), I heard, "You know, I miss him, too," and my heart hurt. So many people would love to be here celebrating you and saying, "Fuckin' Teddy," while they smiled at your Teddyness.

And I know that so many people miss you that I feel selfish most days. I mean, look at Mom and Dad. Talk about the booby prize with just me left.

But I always go back to when we were little and the threat of only having each other someday ... Your sibling is supposed to be your lifetime's longest relationship.

You're still with me in my heart, but what I wouldn't give to see you blow out your candles for real today.

I'm so mad at you, but I love you so much. Happy birthday, you fucking asshole

P.S. I am having a bite of this whoopee pie for breakfast because there are absolutely no rules today.

*****

Grief doesn't have a neat ending. There's no finish line or awesome, blingy medal. There's no "closure" (despite what people say), and no magic moment where everything suddenly makes sense.

It becomes part of you—a thread woven into the fabric of who you are. And while it's not something I'll ever stop carrying, I've found a way to give it a voice. Writing and sharing have become my way of navigating this endless, messy road.

In a way, these letters feel like love letters. They're a way to pour out everything I can no longer say to Teddy in person. They're filled with memories, emotions, and little pieces of our story that only he might understand.

Sometimes, they feel raw and jagged, like all the blues of the ocean after a terrible storm. Other times, they're soft and golden, like younger Teddy's beautiful, angelic hair. No matter the tone, they're my way of keeping him close. They're love with nowhere to go, yet they always find their way onto the page.

I know I'll keep writing these letters for as long as needed. Maybe forever. When I write to Teddy, it feels like a one-sided conversation, but still a connection. I imagine what he'd say back, how he'd laugh, roll his eyes, or tease me for getting too sentimental—because that just isn't me, but it was most definitely him.

And in those moments, he feels less gone ... Present in every way, even if just in the shape of my words.

3

Depression, Anxiety, OCD, and Panic ... Oh My!

I've spent most of my life trying to hide my anxiety, depression, panic attacks, obsessive-compulsive disorder, and more. I didn't want to be the "weird one" (more than I already was) or the person people handled with care. I became an expert at masking—smiling on cue, cracking self-deprecating jokes, excelling at work and school, and doing everything I could to keep people from seeing the cracks beneath the surface.

I shared my feelings with a trusted adult when I was about ten. Looking back, I don't know what I was thinking ... It was the 1980s when no one talked about anything, let alone feelings. Maybe I wanted validation, comfort, or someone to tell me I would be okay. Instead, I heard I didn't know what it meant to feel that way because I had a good life, so stop whining.

So, I did.

This is how I lived for the entirety of my life. I convinced myself that admitting I struggled would make me weak. If I could try to be perfect, work harder, plan better, or get more control over my thoughts, then I'd be fine. I wouldn't need help. I wouldn't have to explain why I felt like I was coming undone, even when everything looked "fine" from the outside.

But grief has a way of shattering illusions. When Teddy died, every carefully constructed mask I had built crumbled. At first, I thought I could write about him—about who he was, what I had lost, and how grief felt like sleepwalking through life.

But as I wrote and shared my journey, something started to feel off. How could I talk about the weight of losing Teddy without acknowledging the weight I had already been carrying for so many years? Especially since the weeks leading up to Teddy's death, I had been stuck in my own depressive episode—one of the deepest I'd experienced in my entire lifetime. It's incredibly difficult for me to admit this, but the week that we lost Teddy to suicide, I had contemplated taking my own life.

Writing about grief while pretending my mental health challenges didn't exist felt disingenuous, like I was only telling part of the story. So, I began to write about it—not all at once and not always in the most graceful way, but that's authentically me.

Side quest!
Because that's how my brain works...

Did you know? In five generations, I have been the only one in my direct ancestral line not to have "Grace" in my name. My maternal great-grandmother was Grace, my grandmother was Jennie Grace, my mother is Mary-Grace, and my daughter is Abigail Grace. I have no Grace, but literally and figuratively. But, to use the phrase that makes my best friend Jenn chortle, I digress ... And, I hope Jenn snort-laughed at the word, "chortle."

In sharing my grief, I started to share my struggles with mental health. I wrote about the panic attacks like the one that found me paralyzed in the middle of the Boston Marathon race expo, the obsessive thoughts that wouldn't let me sleep or kept me trapped each day, the depression that creeps in and sits on my chest sometimes for weeks. I wrote about my experiences with complex post-traumatic stress disorder (cPTSD) and PTSD, and later about my experience with late-diagnosed ADHD, which honestly helped me make sense of so much in my life. I wrote about the ways grief amplified those struggles, turning up the volume on what I had tried so hard to suppress for years.

At first, the thought of being open and candid like this terrified me. What would people think? But something unexpected happened: people began to respond. They thanked me for being honest. They told me they saw themselves in my words. They shared their stories, and I slowly realized I wasn't alone. The more I talked about my mental health, the more others opened up about theirs. Friends, family, and even strangers began to reach out—not just to offer support but to share their struggles or ask for advice on how to help someone they loved.

That's when it hit me: mental illness doesn't always look the way people expect it to. It doesn't come with a neon sign or a flashing warning. Sometimes, it looks like being "high functioning." Sometimes, it looks like being the person others can always rely on. And sometimes, it is sitting in your car, too exhausted to walk into the house, wondering how you'll get through another day.

People think OCD is about being neat and organized, but it's not always. For me, it's intrusive thoughts that I can't escape. For others, they feel compelled to perform rituals even when they don't make sense. People think depression is just being "sad," but it's not always. For me, it's a heaviness that makes everything, even breathing, feel like work. People think anxiety is just worrying too much, but it's not always. For me, it's a constant hum of dread, a buzzing under your skin that you can't shut off.

This chapter exists because we need honest conversations about mental health—conversations that aren't sanitized or simplified. Life isn't "Insta-perfect," nor is grief, healing, or learning to live with a brain that doesn't always cooperate.

I share my story not because I have all the answers. (I have none of the answers, by the way.) I share because I know how isolating it feels to think you're the only one struggling. You're not. And if there's one thing I've learned, there's power in vulnerability. There's power in saying, "This is my reality, and it's complicated, and it's difficult, but I'm still here."

I would love to hear from you if you see some of yourself in the following posts or if something resonates with you. Reach out to me at HealingMiles41@gmail.com. (Yes, I did just give the whole world my email address, Mary-Grace!)

*****

January 7, 2024

I am a total neat freak. Clutter gives me agita (Italian slang for "heartburn"). I live by my Grandma Jennie's rule of never leaving the house with your bed unmade or a dish in the sink.

And when I'm anxious, cleaning helps me expel some extra energy.

But I live with both anxiety and depression. And, when the depression scale tips a little lower than the anxiety scale, you can tell. I sleep A LOT, and things get a tad messy. Usually, one of the most significant signs is my kitchen island. It's typically empty because of, you know, the clutter issue. Last night, however, it was heaped with mail, papers, running stuff, and items for the recycling bin. Every time I walked past it, I felt stressed but did nothing about it.

Thanks to my cat Luna vomiting on the island, we had to clean it off. I thanked Luna for helping me with my depression mess, and I think the family was surprised by that revelation.

Because I need a logical explanation for everything in life, I did a little reading on the topic. Here's what I found:

Depression reduces energy, hindering cleaning and organizing, leading to clutter accumulation.

Depression impairs decision-making and concentration, making prioritizing and initiating tasks like tidying up hard.

Negative emotions in depression intensify during cleaning, leading to task avoidance.

Depression impairs planning and organizing, making it difficult to maintain an organized living space and resulting in clutter.

Depression leads to neglecting self-care, including maintaining a clean living environment, as basic tasks become challenging.

If you find yourself letting things slide when you're not feeling your best, I hope this helps provide some context so you can give yourself grace as you manage through it!

*****

November 20, 2024

I've shared this before, but when my mental health dips, basic self-care gets, um, complicated. I noticed yesterday I hadn't showered since Sunday. Yikes!

The pattern?

There have been no workouts lately (thanks to the ongoing health issues), so there is no reason to shower. I'm not diligent about my hydration or nutrition, so why bother? And then the showers start slipping.

My therapist once gave me a lifeline for days like this: complete three simple tasks—just three, and just simple enough to make me feel a little human again.

Here are mine:

- Eat one nutritious meal. Even if it's just some fruit and yogurt.
- Shower. Or wash my face if a full shower feels impossible. (If you know me, you know that I have zero skincare routine!)
- Go outside for five minutes. Fresh air does something, I swear. It did me wonders yesterday!!!

Need help thinking of a list for yourself? Start tiny. A sip of water. Changing into clean clothes. Still too much? Lie near a window. Let the light in. Be kind to yourself. It ALLLLL counts.

Whatever you're doing, I hope you have an awesome day. And if it's a tough day, I hope you find a few moments of joy.

*****

The Apple TV series, *Physical*, became the subject of more than one post. The main character, Sheila Rubin, lives with an eating disorder and other mental health challenges, carrying a level of self-loathing I thought only existed in my own mind. It was difficult to watch, but for the first time, I felt seen, understood, and represented in a way I never had before. I'm including all the related posts here because they resonated deeply with others, sparking conversations that reminded me I'm not alone in these struggles.

*****

August 26, 2024
Content Warning: Eating Disorder

Last night, I started watching the Apple TV show *Physical*, about a woman in the '80s who finds joy and empowerment in aerobics.

Watching Sheila struggle with an eating disorder and a vicious inner voice was tough—it was like hearing my inner monologue at some points.

I recognized the feeling all too well: SHAME. The shame, bruhhhh-hhh.

When the episode ended, I was almost relieved. Watching Sheila struggle to maintain life while that relentless inner voice tells her over and over that she is wrong and bad, and then watching her binge eat and start the shame cycle over again, hurt my heart.

I'm still deciding whether to keep watching. It's a lot, and (at least in this first episode) it hits too close to home. If I continue watching, it'll be with some breathing space between episodes.

Still, there's something to be said about seeing your battles reflected on screen, making you feel a little less alone in the fight. And what a fight it can be—I'm a tough cookie, but that inner voice wins more often than I'd like to admit.

Today, I choose to be a little bit kinder to myself. I intentionally did not write "kind" to myself because I know the reality, but the little bit is a start.

I hope you can speak kindly to yourself today, too. As my therapist likes to say, your thoughts are not facts!

*****

September 3, 2024

I'm still watching the *Physical*. It's getting easier to watch, kind of. Sheila Rubin's internal monologue could be my own at times.

While filming an aerobics video on the beach, Sheila's self-hatred is LOUD. But what struck me was that she said almost the same things I have said to myself over and over and over again every time I run a race and see myself next to the "natural" runners.

Almost word for word.

"They're all staring at you, heifer. They're all wondering what the fuck you think you're doing. Who the fuck you think you are?"

The only difference between Sheila and myself is that my inner voice uses "fat asshole" in place of "heifer."

Yes, I recognize that this is a cognitive distortion, thanks to a shit ton of therapy. And, even if I don't look like a runner, no one thinks that about me because people are focused on themselves. And, if they are judging me, that's a sad commentary on their character versus my status as an "athlete."

Easier said than believed, though.

Yesterday, a friend reached out after feeling down on herself. She'd been working out consistently but hadn't seen any progress. She felt discouraged, but I saw her posts and continually feel so inspired, and I told her as much!

And I got her message moments after I ran past a row of shops and saw my reflection in the windows ... And berated myself for being "disgusting."

Thank you, Britt, for reminding me to be a little nicer to myself sometimes. (Also, keep moving and inspiring, my sweet friend!)

If you have a vicious inner voice ... Please know you're not alone! And, please understand that the voice is a total liar. You are perfect just as you are. Right this minute.

*****

October 2, 2024

I'm still working my way through *Physical*, and God damn, does it hit close to home sometimes.

The main character, Sheila Rubin, is a tall, lithe, almost impossibly perfect woman on the outside. But inside? It's brutal. Her inner critic is relentless, constantly telling her she's not enough, failing, and not measuring up.

I watched this scene last night, in which her friend Greta drops this phrase in response to Sheila's obsessing over her competition: "Compare and despair."

It hit like a punch. Sheila was spiraling, and Greta just said it so simply, then moved on, like it wasn't even a question.

For people like Sheila (and me), it's often not that simple. When I'm stuck there, feeling like I'm falling short compared to others, all I can think is, "I'll never be good enough, never look like a runner, never have it together the way I'm supposed to." No matter how hard I try, it's never enough to satisfy that voice in my head.

I have a feeling that's why I feel so tired this morning—exhausted to my core, really.

But I also recognize that even though my mug today says so, I do not have correct opinions on everything.

Especially when it comes to myself.

Can you relate? If you can, try one thing today to show yourself the same kindness and compassion that you extend to others.

Not easy, I know. But so worth it.

*****

October 10, 2024

Today is World Mental Health Day ... and it's a good time to remember that everyone has mental health.

Just like physical health, it's something we all deal with, whether or not we have a diagnosed issue.

I was about nine or ten years old the first time I realized that the level of sadness, panic, and nonstop inner critical voice I experienced as my baseline was not the same as that of my neighborhood friends. I didn't have the words to explain it, but now I know them to be depression, anxiety, and OCD. And I've learned a few more words and acronyms along the way.

That's my reality, and I'm not ashamed of it. Therapy is my regular go-to, and I've been through an intensive outpatient program when things got especially hard. It saved my life, and I don't say that lightly.

But you don't need a diagnosis to care about mental health. Just like we care for our bodies, we must also care for our minds.

- One in five adults in the United States has a mental health condition every year.
- 50% of all lifetime mental illnesses begin by age fourteen.
- People with mental health conditions are two times as likely to experience substance use disorders.

And if you need this reminder today: This world needs you.

*****

April 16, 2022

This has been the most fantastic day, and I will still have a late lunch with some of the inspiring Team AFSP runners later this afternoon.

The whole city feels magical, and it should. This is the first time in several years that the Boston Marathon has been run on its traditional Patriots Day holiday.

I even got to have my caricature drawn by someone dear to me, Susan Festa. Sue's son and Jimmy went to elementary school together, and I have always enjoyed her company.

What you don't see in this photo of me at bib pickup is that sneaky panic disorder I wrote about last week. The Adidas booth at the marathon expo was enclosed and crowded. Last year, I had my family to help me navigate, but this year I was alone.

I felt hot and cold, and began seeing spots ... I knew what was coming. I went to a volunteer—by this time, I was shaking, and my vision was blurred. He was incredibly kind and brought me to the head of security, who shared that someone he loves has a similar disorder. The cashier handled me with care and got me out quickly.

I appreciate their kindness more than you can ever imagine.

*****

In early 2023, I experienced something that activated some traumatic memories and left me unable to function daily. Although it was scary to do so, after weeks of declining mental health, I planned to ask my therapist to help me find some more intensive support. Sensing my distress, she asked if I felt like I needed some extra help. I was lucky to get a spot in an intensive outpatient program, which I attended daily for two weeks. I can unequivocally say that this program saved my life.

It also introduced me to Acceptance and Commitment Therapy, or ACT. The premise of ACT is less about challenging overwhelming, negative thoughts, which, for me, only proves to give them more strength, and more about recognizing and sitting with these uncomfortable thoughts, while still moving toward a life aligned with my goals and values.

The following posts are a selection from my time in the program. I have included them in the hope that if you recognize yourself needing extra support, you will reach out and seek it.

*****

May 12, 2023

"The fears that we don't face become our limits." ~ Robin Sharma

To start my day, I ran seven miles in the heat. I went out too fast and paid for it during the back half, but my times during miles one through three were faster than I've been able to do since before the Achilles injury.

I like to think I'm generally fearless. Except when facing that monster who hides in the dark places inside me. The "monster" who still drives the bus despite a lot of therapy and what my therapist called "post-traumatic growth."

It's time to stop trying to avoid facing it. It's time to do what I do best: go all in and face this thing head-on. Like everything, I'm approaching it with cautious optimism and some skepticism. I mean, if I haven't been able to tame the unhelpful thoughts, how is someone who doesn't know me going to fix that? But I'm all in and ready to start that hard work with the tenacity of a Sicilian donkey.

New steps toward healing begin Monday morning.

*****

May 15, 2023

"There is hope, even when your brain tells you there isn't." ~ John Green, *Turtles All the Way Down*

Recognizing the need and asking for help are not among my strongest qualities. Yet, here I am, accepting support and heading into a new opportunity to grow and challenge myself and my unhelpful thoughts.

I can't promise I won't throw a middle finger or two, but I am committed to approaching this with an open mind because I realize that my brain tells me a lot of lies.

*****

May 17, 2023

Today's focus was self-compassion. This is problematic for me; the group leader recognized that I might want to flip him off at some point. I totally wanted to.

But I promised myself to give this my all so I can continue to grow and learn ways to manage anxiety, depression, OCD, ADHD, cPTSD, and PTSD. I'm tired of letting them drive the bus.

So, I went all in, just like I said I would; by the end of the day, I was mentally and physically exhausted.

This run was so needed. I didn't have any expectations beyond a three-mile treadmill run. I felt pretty strong, so I increased the speed to what I did before the injury last fall. I eliminated most intervals, walking only when I needed water and wiping my face.

I am proud of the time, proud of my effort throughout, and proud of myself for not berating myself for not doing more.

*****

May 19, 2023

One piece of this week that I have found helpful is the introduction of ACT therapy.

Whereas I'd previously learned to challenge negative thought patterns with things like positive mantras (guess how well that worked for me?!), ACT focuses on the willingness to recognize the emotions and physical sensations but to use mindfulness and acceptance to live according to one's values (or in pursuit of what is most important).

There are several strategies, but unsurprisingly, I find the rebellious approach most intriguing ... I think of that negative story as a bully and disobey it, even as it continues to run in the back of my mind.

It sounds strange, but I think I can use this and some of the other strategies to help me defuse the unhelpful narrative that has formed some pretty shitty core beliefs.

So, even if I am a horrible person, tough shit. I will continue connecting with people and not isolating myself because relationships are significant.

*****

May 22, 2023

I'm pretty sure I fell asleep within minutes of turning my phone to do not disturb last night, and I slept until Daisy woke me up at five o'clock. After feeding all the animals, I fell back to sleep and just got up to have breakfast before getting ready.

Week two begins today.

Call it a partial hospitalization program (PHP), intensive outpatient program, or whatever you like. I can tell you it was the light in the dark tunnel that I so desperately needed.

To those who have said I hope it fixes you and puts you in a better mood, please stop.

The goal is not to "fix" me. I am not broken. The goal is instead to help me recognize negative thought patterns and develop strategies to manage them alongside anxiety and depression, so I can continue to work through them and the PTSD with my outside therapist. While not the target, I've been able to use what I've learned so far to quiet some of the trauma stuff.

If you're considering a program like this, talk with your therapist or primary care provider. Most have waiting lists, so it's best to get the ball rolling.

*****

May 24, 2023

This morning, I set a goal of completing three miles in thirty-three minutes. I dug deep and came in under that with a 10:50 minute per mile pace.

For me, that is celebration time … Even before all my injuries, I never ran at that speed.

My friend Erica texted, "It's like somehow there's been a weight off your shoulders, and now you're faster. Gee, wonder what that could be … Not literal weight but all the shit you carry around."

She's not wrong.

Learning to accept things (and people) as they are, setting boundaries with myself and others, and challenging negative thought patterns have helped me feel lighter in so many ways. Granted, it's new and exciting, so I'll need to practice these daily.

Likewise, working on grounding and distraction (without becoming constantly busy) can help with PTSD.

I'm so proud of the progress I've made, both physically and mentally.

*****

May 27, 2023

I got my five-mile run yesterday after PHP. The last few weeks have been intense, so I reserved a table at a local restaurant that I enjoy and invited some dear friends to join me for margaritas and dinner.

I've learned that I'd become skilled at wearing a mask with most people, even when depression and anxiety were at their highest levels. But not with these friends—they see me always, and I am lucky to have them in my life.

No mask needed last night, for sure. My cheeks still hurt a little from laughing.

I'm taking my long run today, and it looks like it will be cooler outside than tomorrow. If you see me smiling, I'm thinking about last night.

Another side quest for you …
I've included this post because this dinner has become one of those core memories that I will forever cherish. I know April, Kerri, and Nichole from separate areas of life, and the four of us had never spent time together. Yet, the conversation was easy, and the laughter was, let's say, plentiful. I am also ninety-nine percent sure we ruined a couple's first date with our shenanigans. Ten stars, would do it all over again.

*****

October 18, 2023

In my virtual ACT group yesterday, we completed a self-evaluation on our ability to show ourselves compassion. I knew my score would be low, as this is one of my biggest challenges. I wasn't surprised at all.

I scored 1.38 on a 1-5 scale.

I am, quite literally, my harshest critic.

We talked about ways to better cultivate self-compassion to help us live more fully, and this week's assignment is to write a self-compassionate letter to ourselves.

You know I'm dreading THAT more than anything. My instinct would be to procrastinate and hastily write something in the twenty minutes before the next group.

For my own accountability, I'm committing to writing it on Sunday. I've even scheduled time in my calendar with a reminder.

It would probably be easier to attempt a one-hundred-mile run than it will be to write this shit, but reminding myself: I'm stronger than I think, and stronger than I feel.

*****

As I look back on the posts I've shared in this chapter, I realize they're not just reflections on my mental health—they're markers of growth. They document the shift from hiding to embracing, from masking to letting myself be seen. Sharing these struggles wasn't part of my plan, but it became an unintended and necessary step in my grief (and life) journey.

These posts, like grief itself, aren't linear or neat. They're raw, sometimes uncomfortable, and deeply personal. But sharing doesn't just lighten my load. It also creates space for others to feel safe sharing theirs. Every time someone reaches out to say, "I feel that too," or "You helped me put words to something I couldn't explain," it reinforces why this kind of openness and vulnerability matters.

If these posts resonate with you, I hope they remind you that it's okay to struggle, not to have all the answers all the damn time, and to take it one day, hour, minute, or even second at a time. Being open about what's hard and reaching out for help is one of the bravest things someone can do.

If you or someone you love are in crisis, call or text 9-8-8 in the United States, or one of the hotlines shared in the resource section of this book.

4

Body Like a Battle-Scarred Warrior
(And Learning to Love It Anyway)

I never set out to become a runner. If you had told me years ago that I would one day be running marathons across the country, I would have laughed my giant, loud laugh that causes my kids to shush me when we're out in a public setting. Running wasn't something I thought about, and certainly not something I ever saw as a part of my identity.

The last time I ran in the time BEFORE was as part of my high school cross country team. That was 1990. A lifetime ago. While we had several talented runners on the team, most of us showed up but didn't expect much else. Our coach, Sister Nancy—a Catholic nun with a thick Boston accent—was a force of nature, full of determination and faith that we'd eventually amount to something as runners.

Sis-tah, as we called her in our own Boston accents, had her own special coaching method. She didn't just encourage us from the sidelines; she ran behind us during practice to ensure we didn't duck into the cemetery and hitch a ride back to school. And let me tell you, more than a few of us had considered it. Running was torture, plain and simple. I hated it with a fiery passion. But I loved the freedom of being with my teammates and driving home afterward, unsupervised, with my friends.

When my final season ended, so did my running career—or so I thought.

Fast forward a few decades, and here I am, not just running around the block but running marathons. So what changed? What would make someone who swore off running lace up their shoes again, not just for a quick jog, but for twenty-six miles and beyond?

Grief changed me. When Teddy died, every carefully constructed piece of my life fell apart. I was stuck in survival mode, barely holding it together for my kids and my job. Stuffing my feelings down with food, shopping, and nights spent staring at the ceiling. I gained nearly 100 pounds in the three years after losing Teddy and slept maybe one or two hours a night. My mental and physical health were at their lowest. Yet, I wasn't able to help myself. I was frozen in the in-between of living and not living.

Enter the COVID-19 pandemic.

My coping mechanisms, which had thrived on secrecy, suddenly became impossible with everyone home all the time. Anxiety buzzed in my chest like a live wire. One day, I knew I needed to escape before I exploded. I put a leash on my dog Penelope, laced up an old pair of sneakers, and walked to the end of my street. I'm embarrassed to admit that it wasn't even a tenth of a mile, and I struggled. Panting, sweating, and muttering under my breath about how much I hated it. And swearing out loud at my brother for leaving me to figure life out without him.

But when I got home, something had shifted. I wasn't "better," but I felt different—like the tight grip of grief had loosened just a little bit. So, I went again the next day. And then again. What started as walking turned into running. Not fast, not graceful, but moving forward. Step by step.

Running has become one of the most powerful tools in my mental health toolkit. It forces me to be present in a way nothing else does. It quiets my racing thoughts, clears the fog of anxiety, and helps me process the chaos of heartbreak. But it hasn't been easy.

I live without a spleen, which means even minor illnesses can knock me out for weeks. I ruptured my Achilles tendon during the Chicago Marathon, a setback that tested my patience in ways I didn't think possible. Stress triggers recurring shingles outbreaks, and my recent hospitalization was another reminder of how unpredictable my body can be.

My legs, bigger than the "average" runner's or the feminine ideal, have carried me through all of it. They are strong, just like me.

I don't fit the mold of the "typical" runner. I'm heavier than most distance runners. I'm not fast, and I'll never win a race. But every mile I run reminds me that I'm still here. Every finish line reminds me that I am capable of more than I ever believed. Running isn't about fitness for me. It's about survival.

It has also taught me patience, something I've had to develop the hard way. (Though, if you know me in real life, then you know that the hard way is the *only* way I learn anything.). Injury, illness, setbacks—they've all forced me to slow down, to listen to my body, and to respect its limits.

And then there's the community.

I didn't expect to meet so many incredible people through running, but I have. My entire circle of friends looks different from that time BEFORE, when I was constantly worried about fitting in ... From the larger running community to my Team AFSP teammates—runners who lace up not just for themselves but to honor loved ones lost to suicide. These connections have transformed me, reminding me I don't have to carry my grief alone.

Running hasn't erased my grief, but it has given me a way to carry it. Some days, I run with the weight of loss pressing down on me, step after step. Other days, I run with a lightness I never thought I'd feel again. No matter how I feel when I start, I always finish knowing one thing: movement is survival. Running is how I navigate grief, one mile at a time.

And every race I run, no matter the distance, ends the same way—saving that final mile for Teddy. I say his name out loud more often than not, and sometimes even, "Let's fucking do this, Asshole!" And, with every step, I imagine his laugh, terrible jokes, and unwavering belief in me, even on my worst days. That last mile is sacred, a quiet moment where it's just me and my brother, together again in a way that feels as real as it is heartbreaking. It's not just a mile; it's my love for him, love that has nowhere else to go.

Looking back, I think of Sister Nancy and her faith in my younger self. The way she'd come up behind me during the final mile and shout, "Push it, Fusco!" Maybe she saw something I couldn't back then. Maybe she knew that running would become part of my identity one day. I'll never know for sure. But I like to think she'd be proud. She might even laugh at the irony of it all.

I never set out to be a runner. But here I am, chasing healing one mile at a time—with legs that carry me like the battle-scarred warrior I've become, and a final mile always dedicated to the brother who taught me how to keep moving forward, even when it feels impossible.

Thank you for running every single mile with me, Fuckin' Teddy. I love you.

******

July 11, 2021

My only goal was to finish the Narragansett Summer Running Festival 10K (my first running race since high school), and I did! I wasn't fast, and it wasn't pretty, but I surprised even myself.

I'd told my family they didn't need to come, which I regretted when tears rose at the starting line. In that moment, looking at runners chasing goals together and supportive families and friends, I felt so incredibly alone ... This reminded me of Teddy, leaving me to do life without him. I texted my best friend, Jenn, and she helped me feel seen and understood.

Seeing friendly faces at mile three was both shocking and motivating. Thank you, Vicki and Tammi!

Next weekend's scheduled long run is 8 miles, and I think I'll be able to do it. Rachel said she thinks I'm stubborn enough to do anything I put my mind to—I tend to agree, and for once, it was good to be my Sicilian donkey self.

*****

October 10, 2021

What you can't see in the pictures is the sweat dripping down my neck from the near-crippling panic attack. Crowds, noise, and impostor syndrome to the millionth degree. It was not pretty.

Wondering if I should even be here. Intellectually, I know no one was looking at me, judging because I'm overweight and not a "real runner." But when I tried on the iconic Boston Marathon celebration jacket, I almost fainted because I felt like I didn't earn the right to be among all these amazing athletes. Felt like everyone was looking and laughing at the chubby mom trying on jackets meant for marathoners.

Tomorrow, THE marathon. Finding my inner donkey so I can complete this race through sheer will, pushed along by Teddy's voice telling me, "Run, Jenny." In his Forrest Gump voice.

NOTE: I am still in disbelief that I did not write a post recapping my very first Boston Marathon, but this post from the day before accurately captures how I feel at most races ... Big, other, too much, not enough. And then I do the thing, and those big legs carry me across miles and miles and miles.

*****

November 23, 2021

This morning, it was below freezing! This weather is my jam. I ran at a leisurely pace, followed by three 15-second strides. I felt slow until an older gentleman walking down Bay Street with a cane yelled, "Holy Smokes, look at you go!"

It's all perspective, like when I did 3x 45-second planks for Erin's plank challenge today. Time literally stood still.

My coach likes to call Tuesdays "transformation Tuesdays." Today's transformation is all mental—even just six months ago, I wouldn't have left the house in anything brightly colored. I was worried that someone would make fun of the chubby mom running.

Yes, people have done that ... While I was training for Boston, some kid riding a bike yelled out, "KEEP RUNNING, CHUBBY MAMA!" and I ran back to say good morning and to offer to let him join me on my twenty-mile long run the following weekend. I think he shit his pants. Totally worth it.

So today I went out in my loud Boston Marathon running set and didn't give a rat's ass who looked at me and laughed. Because I'm moving and I'm getting healthier every day.

*****

October 13, 2022

"You are shut down." This is totally not how I expected the orthopedic visit to go ... The good news is that my ankle is NOT fractured. The bad news is that it is a partial rupture of my Achilles tendon.

This was one of those few doctors who GETS it and understands why I NEED to run and move. And, while he admittedly doesn't want to see me in jail, he also said I could sit out now or end up never running again.

So today, I chose HARD. I messaged Coach Elena Green (Coach E) and will begin reworking my meal plan. I am researching upper body workouts. I am going to slow down and actually accept help.

This is difficult, but just a minor setback. I can make this time what I choose it to be.

I know that Teddy would be the first one at my house, offering to help me, simultaneously driving me up the wall. Don't worry, Teddy. I'm one bad bitch. I'll be running again in no time, and you and Joey can continue to wait for the day I shit my pants while running. As Joey said, it would be EPIC.

*****

December 4, 2022

I joined an online running group, the Misfit Runners, a little over a year ago. Many other online running groups left me feeling pretty uncomfortable, thanks to pace shaming and elitist attitudes. Not the Misfit Runners. Their vibe was about come-as-you-are attitudes, tasteless memes, and middle fingers. From day one, I knew I'd found my people. I've had the good fortune to meet many for races or get-togethers in real life.

Today, fellow Misfits Natalia and Phil joined me in running the Frosty Half Marathon despite my recent challenges. They could've gone ahead (I told them to!), but they stayed with me until the end. I am so ridiculously appreciative.

After an Achilles injury, shingles, and pneumonia, I was a little worried today would end with a DNF (did not finish), but it didn't. I'm sore. And I needed my inhaler (just once).

We were DEAD LAST, but we covered the exact 13.1 miles as the guy who won the race. Our medals are just as shiny. After the race, they joined me for a celebratory lunch with two other Misfits, Carrie and Shereen.

I feel so lucky to have met these folks, and it's heavy knowing I never would have met them had Teddy not died. Today felt like a beautiful gift from my brother. Thank you, Teddy.

*****

April 11, 2024

Raining during my lunch break, and I'm still wiped out, so I'm conserving energy for Saturday's Newport Half Marathon.

So, instead of sharing this updated photo of me from Orlando this January, I've added a crown because, well, who doesn't need one?

And also because in one of my running groups, there was a snarky comment about THICC women and the need to be "thinner."

Awwwww, helllllll no.
Hold my hoops situation for sure.
You. Be. You. Thiccccc or not.

It's taken me a long time to accept my body shape as who I am. To not hide it under bigger clothes.

I am strong … The strongest I've ever been. And healthy (well, except for the shingles hahahahahahahaha). These big legs carry me across soooooo many miles. And they give me a little more room for even more tattoos.

Don't let anyone else tell YOU what you should look like. Be you and love yourself as best you can.

And, as I wrote in my response, if anyone doesn't like my ample derrière, then they can kiss it.

*****

October 5, 2023

I'll never qualify for anything. I'm a back-of-the-pack runner. I don't look like a runner.

AND

I've completed the Boston Marathon, and I'm one of the few who can say they did it twice in six months (October 2021 and April 2022).

I never give up, even when I know I'm beat (hello, limping the final eight miles of the Chicago Marathon with a partial Achilles rupture).

I work every day, even if I never qualify, place, or win my age group.

I follow runners of all abilities and speeds, inspired by each and every one of them daily. I don't envy the things each has achieved because I know they've put in the work. They motivate me to keep going.

I'm only competing with myself, and that woman is a pretty stubborn bitch.

*****

October 9, 2023

A friend shared this photo of me from yesterday, as I was running around the bend toward the finish line.

I don't usually share race photos because I usually cry when I see them. I typically focus on my bigger size and what's wrong with me.

My first thought when I looked at this photo was, "I look strong!"
And I feel strong.

I also look happy and confident, and I definitely felt both yesterday.
Running along the ocean around the midpoint, I remember thinking
about how lucky I was to run this race and see these views. Yes, it meant
leaving my house by 5 a.m. and weeks of training. But I wasn't even
planning on this race. I added it last weekend and hoped to use it as the
week's long run. And what an amazing fucking long run it was!

In those final few miles, when I usually yell for Teddy to help me to
the end, I just thought, "Fuckin' Teddy, we DID this!"

When I talked with Justin and Robbie during the *Golden Hours Adventures Podcast*, co-host Robbie commented on all the runs I do in
memory of others and asked, "When will you do a race just for you?"
I remember feeling surprised by the question. It's not something I ever
considered.

Robbie, thank you for giving me that gift. Yesterday was for me, and
I loved every single minute of it.

*****

November 4, 2023

I am officially an ultramarathoner!

After almost thirteen hours at the Hamsterwheel endurance race in New Hampshire, I completed ten loops for a total of forty miles.

When I finished, I once again almost cried—tears of joy. This is not something I could have ever dreamed of doing, and yet I did it.

It is bittersweet knowing I would never have started running without losing Teddy. I thanked him and yelled, "Fuckin' Teddy!" when I finished.

The Hamsterwheel was a perfect first endurance race, with its four-mile loop. I stopped after each one to refill my water bottle or have a snack ... The food was ridiculously good—I'm a big fan of the grilled cheese.

The atmosphere was better than anything I could have imagined, and the sense of community was unparalleled. I never felt so welcomed at a race as I did today!

I am going to bed (after I eat some Funyuns in bed) with a happy and grateful heart.

*****

June 22, 2024

Gary Bjorklund Half Marathon during Grandma's Marathon is complete! Hands down, the highlight of the race was mile seven.

I heard some weirdo behind me say, "I like your shirt." I turned to give him my best resting bitch face, but it was Dave Thompson, from AFSP Minnesota—and also one of my most favorite humans.

Right there, we saw a family giving out cups of beer and stopped, even though it was definitely not a great idea. We toasted our siblings, Teddy and Katherine, for whom we run.

This second part of life—the time after—has been filled with so much sadness. But meeting fellow loss survivors like Dave has shown me that joy and grief can coexist.

Thank you, Dave. (P.S., I still want matching tattoos!)

*****

October 13, 2024
Jenny's first DNF

It was not the race finish I expected. Around mile seven, I started to feel dizzy, and my vision blurred.

I stopped at the water stop to say I wasn't feeling well, but my lips were blue, and I wasn't making sense.

The EMTs were genuinely kind, even when I refused transport to the hospital. My blood pressure was way too low.

I've been burning the candle at both ends between work, volunteering, training, and life. I haven't felt right since last weekend, but was trying to power through. But, as usual, my body had other ideas.

Stopping and asking for help was difficult, but I know it was the right choice.

I am still disappointed in myself and feel that I let myself and those I was carrying down.

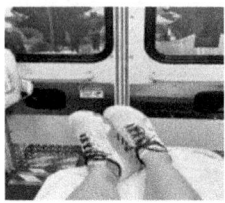

*****

October 14, 2024

Yesterday's DNF at the Newport Marathon was a huge wake-up call. I've been burning the candle at both ends—and, honestly, in the middle too—doing too much, pushing through, and ignoring the signs my body has been throwing at me for weeks.

For those who don't know, I had my spleen removed so I wouldn't need regular blood transfusions, but I still live with hereditary spherocytosis. When I'm run down, my body literally just stops working right.

Even though I post daily about how it's okay to not be okay, I still considered pushing through. Asking for help at the water stop was one of the hardest decisions I've ever made, and also the right one.

The support and love I've received since then has been incredible. A DNF might sting, but it's NOT a failure. As one friend so kindly (and hilariously) reminded me,

"Bitch, your lips were blue!"

I mean, she's not wrong! My body was giving me all the signals that rest was not just an option—it was mandatory.

Another friend hit me with some real talk: "Joey doesn't want to wipe your butt for the rest of your life because you passed out and slammed your head on a curb." As much as I love running, I'm not signing up for that.

It's incredible how many other runners opened up and shared their own DNF stories with me—some about times they stopped and how proud they were of themselves, and others about those times they should have stopped. One friend told me about a marathon where she literally pooped herself at mile fifteen but kept going anyway. She spent days afterward in bed, horribly sick, all because she felt like she had to finish. It was a reminder that we've all pushed our bodies beyond what's safe, and sometimes the bravest thing we can do is stop when we know we should.

So, here's the lesson I'm taking away: It's okay to stop. It's okay to ask for help. And it's okay to prioritize your health, even if it means missing out on the finish line. The finish line will be there next time—and so will I.

*****

November 13, 2024

I'm sure you're not surprised by this, but I NEVER wanted to be the PRINCESS. I always wanted to be the ONE WITH THE SWORD.

> Can we please stop calling women "ma'am?" I fucking hate it. When I walk in somewhere, I want to hear "excuse me, badass, how can I help you?" We've been around, seen some shit, and keep it all going. Badass. From now on. Spread the word.

When I saw this meme last night, I immediately shared it because, damn straight, I identify as a tough cookie.

EVEN IF right now I'm feeling significantly less than badass-y.

Let's paint this picture for you, Bob Ross. It's TOTALLY HOT.

I'm connected to oxygen all the time now. There's an alarm on the bed so I don't try to get up again (let's say it was a big fail). And because of the no-walk thing, I'm wearing a hot external catheter AND a massive Depends ...

I know, you're thinking SO HOT. (Though I will admit, when I saw the Depends, my first thought was, "That'd be awesome for a race.")

Back to the meme ... My friends responded appropriately, agreeing to only call me Badass from now on. Well, except the Southerners. The best they promised was Dude or "Yes, ma'am, your badassness."

But my favorite was from fellow Misfit Runner Rhett:

"Jen, her Highness Queen of the Realm, Commander of the Raccoon Army, Babe of the Babe-lonians, and Badass."

I wonder if that will fit on my next race bib. Oh, because, yeah, kihh-hhhd, there WILL BE a next race.

I shit you not.

Because I'm a tough Sicilian donkey, I will run and throw middle fingers again soon.

I am thankful to all of my circle for keeping me snort laughing through this ridiculous catastrophe. You're the real badasses.

*****

November 30, 2024

It's been forty-eight days since I last ran.

I miss the meditative nature of running. I miss the challenge and proving to myself that yes the fuck I can. And I miss the extra calories.

I've gained about seven pounds. My core and legs have become softer. My pants are tight.

This has been a true test of all that I've learned to manage the intrusive thoughts that accompany OCD. The absolutely vile things that my inner voice tells me ... Things I wouldn't say to even my worst enemy.

Fat
Gross
Ugly
Unlovable
Worthless
Stupid

My inner voice tells me that my size dictates my worth and level of intelligence—you know, things that are totally connected.

And then, while I was doom scrolling Instagram, I saw a carousel post of a beautiful woman wearing just a bra and panties—each image contained thoughts on how we are more than our outward appearance, why body shaming (externally and internally) damages us, and how the "feminine ideal" is seldom achievable (outside of genetics) without intense activity or plastic surgery.

I felt her words. She said to me what I would say to a friend feeling the same way.

But it was more than that.

She was absolutely beautiful, and her body was softer: wide hips, thick thighs, and tummy rolls. Her body resembled mine in so many ways.

Yet she looked comfortable in her body, something I have never experienced.

I didn't scoff at her photos or call her fat, gross, ugly, worthless, unlovable, or stupid because none of those things are true.

I tried to go back later and find the post so I could save and share it, but of course, it was lost in the algorithm somewhere. So, instead, I'm writing about it so that next year, it pops up in my memories as a reminder that I am worthy of love and acceptance. Always.

And so are you.

*****

At the time of writing, I have recovered from the mysterious illness that landed me in the hospital and on the sidelines for months. That "freak virus" was a true test of patience for me, and I feel like I was able to draw on all of my prior experiences to show me that I'd made it through difficult times before, and I would once again.

Running has become my way of living with loss, a way to carry grief without letting it crush me. It's not an escape; it's a declaration of my love for my brother and of myself, of my own independence, and more. With every step, I remind myself—and the world—that I'm still here, still moving forward, even when it feels impossible.

That final mile has become sacred for me. It's not just a part of the run; it's a deliberate act of love and remembrance. That mile belongs to Teddy. It's for him, and it's for me, too. I don't just say his name during that mile. It's my way of telling him, "You're still here, Teddy. You're still with me." That mile gives me purpose when I feel like I have none. It's my way of channeling love that has nowhere else to go.

But running isn't just about Teddy. It's also about me—accepting who I am, scars (both visible and invisible) and all. My body, far from anyone's idea of perfection, has carried me through illness, injury, and moments where I doubted I could go on. These legs, bigger than the so-called runner's ideal, are a testament to resilience. They're strong. They've taken me places I never dreamed I'd go. And they've taught me that my worth isn't tied to how I look, but to what I've survived.

This journey has been messy, like most everything in my life. I've faced ruptured tendons, recurring shingles, and illnesses that knocked me out for weeks. I've pushed through the physical and emotional pain of being a runner who doesn't fit the mold. There have been tears, setbacks, and times when I wanted to give up. But every time I lace up, I choose to keep moving. Not because it's easy, but because it matters.

Running reminds me that progress isn't always linear, but forward is forward.

And along the way, I've found a community of people who inspire and support me. Some of them are fellow runners; others are part of Team AFSP, honoring loved ones lost to suicide. These connections have shown me that grief doesn't have to be a solitary journey. There's strength in leaning on others, sharing the load, and celebrating the small victories along the way.

I didn't plan this chapter of my life, but I've fully embraced it. Running has given me a way to honor Teddy, heal my heart, and rediscover who I am. It's taught me patience, resilience, and the power of showing up—even when it's hard.

To quote Teddy's Favorite movie, *Forrest Gump*: "I don't know if we each have a destiny, or if we're all just floating around accidental-like on a breeze. But I think maybe it's both. Maybe both are happening at the same time."

5

How Running Fixed Me,
Except When It Didn't

People love a good transformation story, and I'm no exception.

You know, the kind where someone hits rock bottom or has all the odds stacked against them. Then, thanks to a breakthrough moment or relationship, they rise from the ashes—stronger, better, healed ... A winner in life. The kind where there's a clear turning point—the struggle is neatly resolved, tied up with a perfect, inspiring bow.

I hate to break it to you, but this isn't that.

While I'll never be speedy, no matter how far or fast I run, I can't outrun my grief.

I can't outrun the anxiety that has lived in me long before Teddy died, or the depression that settled in my core after losing him. I can't outrun the guilt, the "what ifs," or the overwhelming exhaustion of pretending I was okay when I am not.

For a while, though, I thought running would be my transformation story. If I ran far, fast, or long enough, I could rebuild myself into someone unbreakable. I would be able to run my way out of grief, depression, and the aching absence Teddy left behind.

And for a while, it felt like it was working.

Running gave me structure when everything else in my life had fallen apart. It forced me out of bed on mornings when the weight of loss felt too heavy. It gave me a way to channel the rage, the sadness, the endless loop of survivor's guilt. Running helped me feel like I was in control of something, even while my entire world was upside down and shattered.

I told myself that running was fixing me.

If I kept going, I would eventually find the version of myself that didn't feel shattered anymore. And to some extent, running did help me heal. It gave me purpose when I felt lost. It introduced me to a community of people who understood grief, mental health struggles, and the way movement can become survival.

But, again, this isn't a neat, tidy transformation story because some things can't be outrun.

There were days when I set out on my planned run, only to find myself sobbing on the sidewalk, unable to take another step. There were races where I crossed the finish line expecting triumph, only to feel empty. Sometimes, running felt more like punishment than relief—it wasn't fixing me but exposing how broken I was. And, to be perfectly honest, I welcomed the punishment. I craved it.

I thought running would be the thing that saved me, but it couldn't. Because grief isn't something you fix. And mental health isn't something you muscle through with sheer willpower.

Still, running gave me something I didn't realize I needed: proof that I could keep going, even when it was hard.

It didn't erase the pain, but it gave me a place to put it. It didn't eliminate the days when I felt stuck, but it reminded me that movement was possible, even if it was slow or didn't look like what I wanted it to.

Running didn't save me. But it did carry me through. It taught me patience, something I've never been great at. It taught me how to sit with discomfort and keep moving even when things feel impossible. Some days, the miles come easily. Other days, every step is a battle.

But no matter what, I keep going, stubborn like the Sicilian donkey I am.

And at the end of every race, I save the final mile for Teddy. Not because I think he's watching, not because I believe it will ever make up for losing him, but because it's mine to give. That mile is my love, my grief, my way of saying, "I'm still here. I'm still moving ... We are still here. We are still together."

A fellow Team AFSP runner and sibling loss survivor sent me something she wrote that speaks to the heart of why we run:

We Run
By Guadalupe Aguilar
shared with permission

We don't run to break records; we run to break the cycle of silence; we run to manage our mental health.

We run.

We cry out the names of those we have lost to suicide.

We run and push out all of the pain we have inside.

We run, and we share our losses to connect with someone, anyone struggling with mental health.

We run and carry our brothers with us. And in those last few miles, when we feel like we can't go another mile, we think of them, and somehow they carry us to that finish line.

The most important thing we can do, though, is to talk. To break the stigma that surrounds mental health and suicide.

Together, we make a difference—every single day.

We run.

******

These posts—both triumphs and breakdowns—paint the complete picture of what running has meant to me. It hasn't fixed me, but it's carried me through, and will continue to be a massive piece of my mental health toolbox for as long as my body allows.

*****

October 12, 2021, at the Boston Marathon Finish Line

At mile 25, my pace slowed wayyyy down, and I walked a little. I passed a few runners receiving medical care. I worried that I wouldn't finish, even with just one mile to go.

I saw a woman holding a sign that read, "Remember your why." I thought of my brother Teddy, of AFSP, of Healing Miles, and all of my family and friends.

And I did what I did in March 2020, when I couldn't even walk to the end of the street and back. I yelled out, "LET'S FUCKING GO, TEDDY!"

It was little more than a shuffle, but I was able to propel myself forward in a half-jog. Buoyed by the screaming crowd and the magic that is the Boston Marathon, I was able to finish strong (for me), with my family's smiling faces being the last thing I saw before I crossed that famous yellow-and-blue finish line.

Thank you, Teddy.

*****

June 17, 2023, in Duluth, Minnesota

Teddy, we did it!

On a scale of one to ten, today was a total thirteen-point-FUN!

People told me that Grandma's Marathon weekend was beautiful and amazing, but I couldn't appreciate it until I saw it myself. Everyone here is SO NICE. Teddy, we're not in Boston anymore!

I finished faster than I'd hoped, slowing down only during one mile when there was a lawn display of people lost to suicide. I stopped to take photos and to think about them, and those I carried with me today.

What. A. Day.

******

March 18, 2024, in Virginia Beach, Virginia

I am a huge believer in signs. I don't know whether they're real or not, but they help me continue feeling connected to my brother.

Dragonflies. Monarch butterflies. Random words. And, of course, Blue Jays.

I'd stop to pick up Blue Jay feathers during my summer trail runs. I'd keep them in the side pocket of my hydration vest and then add them to a bowl I have at home.

During the Yeungling Shamrock Half Marathon yesterday, I took my phone out of the same pocket to capture the moment—at the beginning of the final mile—when I told Teddy, "Let's fucking get this done!"

I felt something stuck between my fingers and saw a forgotten summer trail run Blue Jay feather.

Teddy was never subtle in life, so it's unsurprising that he continues to bring me signs with the gentleness of a wrecking ball.

I teared up a little, but definitely laughed more—and said aloud, "Thanks, jerk."

When I got to the finish line, my cheeks hurt from smiling.

And, of all the pranks that Teddy ever played on me, turning me into a runner has to be the best.

*****

June 13, 2024

I woke up thinking I had a tummy ache. It turned out I had sore stomach muscles after running the furthest distance since late May, ha ha ha.

I've been procrastinating on a whole bunch of stuff, but this past week I had to make sure travel details were finalized for my second Grandma's Marathon weekend in Minnesota. NEXT WEEK.

I think at least part of my delay was anxiety.

Last year, I had a big PR (personal record) at this race and spent an afternoon creating core memories with fellow loss survivor and teammate Dave.

With everything happening in my life right now, I know I'm not getting a PR this time. I'll be happy to finish and enjoy every moment.

But then I also get stuck in that trap.

Looking at photos from last year to see how terrible I look now in comparison

Analyzing my average pace times and listing out the finish times for all of the half marathons I've run

Comparing myself to FAST runners, THIN runners, and everyone

Reminding me that I'm too big to run, gross; not a real runner; less than. Always that I'm less than. Not deserving of happiness or love or even contentment.

Logically, I know this is all untrue. But those sneaky pathways in my brain—worn smooth by decades of telling myself this stuff—are easy and comfortable to ride.

Reminding myself today:

I'm strong. And I'll finish this race, even if it's slow. Because I've got a bit of grit and donkey in me.

Carrying my brother and others along those Healing Miles brings my heart peace—it was never about a finish time, a PR, or placing in my age group.

This will be my sixteenth half marathon since August of 2021 ... I think that makes me a "real" runner.

*****

January 22, 2024

I love my "Mondays are for Marathons" coffee mug. It's a reminder of the very first Boston Marathon that I completed and a great way to look ahead to the week to come. It's no secret that I love Mondays and all of their possibilities.

The week after any race is tough for me, and I've read the same from so many runners. It's a bit of a letdown after training so hard for an event, and then it happens and, poof, all done. Now what?

I've grappled with the post-achievement blues and have found that a few things help ... (which applies to running and regular life!)

Set new goals and find activities that bring joy and purpose.

Surround yourself with a supportive community and share experiences with others.

Take care of your mental health through activities that bring joy and establish self-care routines.

I've already got my next race (OK, maybe a few races) on the calendar, and I have scheduled the next four weeks of training.

This weekend, spending time with other runners I'd only ever met online was a great experience. And sharing my journey with other suicide loss survivors has been even more meaningful.

******

November 30, 2022

I highlighted a passage in the book *Depression Hates a Moving Target* by Nita Sweeney last night. She writes:

"Despite the overall benefits of running, my emotions continued to cycle ... Whenever I saw a stranger sitting in a car on our street, I assumed the person was casing our house ... Other days I shopped uncontrollably for running clothes, then grimaced at the stack of price tags accumulating on the dresser."

God damn, did I feel seen, seen as fuckkkkkk.

I got to thinking about the past six weeks. They started out rocky with the post-marathon blues (yes, it's a real thing) and that pesky Achilles injury. Then, it snowballed into shingles, postherpetic neuralgia, and finally, this ridiculous pneumonia.

I missed the final race of the Boston Athletic Association distance medley.

I won't be running the Frosty half for my birthday.

Jimmy traveled to Italy (his first trip alone).

And another Thanksgiving without Teddy.

Given my depression, anxiety, catastrophic thinking, compulsive tendencies, AND not running, I could easily have been in the midst of a full-blown crisis by now.

But I'm not, and I am proud of my progress and incredibly thankful for my extended support system.

Was it perfect? Nope. But was it a dramatic improvement from prior situations? Abso-fucking-lutely.

There's always going to be work that needs doing, but I know it's important also to stop sometimes to acknowledge some of the really heavy shit we can carry.

******

May 11, 2023

Yesterday's run—four solid treadmill miles at lunchtime. I felt strong throughout and look forward to a shorter run today and a long one tomorrow.

An online running friend, a therapist, recommended an episode of The Running Explained podcast, "Running Isn't Therapy." I listened while I ran and loved every second of it.

I've said many times that running is an important piece of my mental health toolbox, but it is not my only tool. I've done some hard work with help from therapy, with so much more yet to go.

But, I have found myself considering physical activity and non-rest as a coping skill ... Which it's not, and just listening to this opened my mind ways running can be therapeutic, but is NOT a substitute for therapy, and in some cases can exacerbate mental illness symptoms.

They chatted about mindfulness and the importance of cultivating non-running self-care tools.

Some ideas to focus on mindfulness:

Reading or journaling

Meditation and spiritual self-care (could be prayer, being out in nature, or anything to connect to your higher power)

Yoga, stretching, or breathing exercises

Tech-free time

Stillness is difficult for me. It's a sure sign that I need to lean into it to strengthen that muscle.

*****

December 15, 2022

Depression is a sneaky bitch. Just one day after I congratulated myself for accepting that joy and grief could coexist, I woke up feeling off. Nothing specific jumped out at me; I felt a shift in my energy and myself.

This episode feels more potent than others, and it bothers me that I can't pinpoint a specific reason. But that's the thing about depression, anxiety, and mental illness: while a situation might spark certain feelings, these are illnesses like other physical ailments. They impact the brain.

I realized yesterday that I haven't showered since Sunday. Yes, it's awful, but I simply don't have the energy to do so—I wash up and make myself presentable, but I'd rather sleep on the couch than get ready for the day.

My sleep patterns are off. I'm either sleeping before the birds roost at night, awake into the wee hours, or both. I need sleep meds to help me fall asleep because my brain won't stop whirring.

I haven't worked out or moved my body since Sunday. Exercise has become an essential tool in my mental health toolbox, so not working out and not being injured is not a good sign.

The most alarming is that I have not had an appetite at all (I'm usually an emotional eater), and I fell into some self-destructive patterns that I thought I'd put in my rear-view mirror.

Yet, amid this, I've had quite a productive week at home and work.

I share this not for you to worry, but to show you:

It's ok not to be ok.

Smiles (and middle fingers) don't tell a complete story.

It's okay to get help. (I am thankful I have therapy this week!)

It will get better.

Don't worry—I'll shower today. I have Joey's school band concert tonight, and Abby is coming home for winter break!

*****

July 10, 2024, Teddy's 49th birthday

I went out for a five-mile run in 90°F heat because I told myself I needed to feel the road under my feet. But we all know it was to punish myself. I'm really good at that.

Do you remember that word my runner friend coined? I was totally

...

SADSTURBATING

After three and a half miles, I burst into tears and couldn't take one more step, so I sat down on Court Street and sobbed.

Because I'm tired. So. Damn. Tired.

Then, a fellow AFSP board member called me and showed me the kindness I needed. Thank you.

My sister-friend Vicki came to drive me home, but not before she sat on the stairs in the middle of Court Street and hugged me while I cried, even though I was drenched in sweat and smelled like the rotting carcass of a water buffalo.

Vicki even offered to do a dance party for me to Teddy's favorite tunes. She asked me what songs he liked and, like a toddler, told her I didn't care because Teddy is an asshole for leaving me.

Thanks for delivering me home, Vicki. Thanks for listening to me cry and for dealing with my sweaty stench. I love you.

*****

November 17, 2023

I'm more tired this week than I was after the Hamsterwheel ultramarathon. Maybe it's because I only ran four miles last week? Maybe it's because I had a volunteer commitment? Or maybe my nutrition coach, Elena Green, is trying to unalive me with this reduced-calorie goal? Or just because?

It's difficult to accept myself without always being productive, and sitting still is incredibly uncomfortable. I know many who struggle with this, too.

I've heard this called productivity shame—feeling like you've never done enough and that you aren't "allowed" to do unproductive things.

Oooof, that description is a gut hit for me. Does it resonate with you?

Want another gut check?

Brene Brown said, "Shame is the most powerful, master emotion. It's the fear that we're not good enough."

And that's the thing.

YOU ARE ENOUGH. JUST AS YOU ARE RIGHT NOW.

If you struggle with this, here are a few suggestions. I'm trying. (Not always succeeding but always trying. And that's enough.)

Separate your self-worth from your productivity or achievements
Set realistic goals
Appreciate progress over achievement
Not easy stuff to do, but I believe in us!

******

I used to think that if I ran far enough, fast enough, long enough, I'd leave grief, anxiety, and depression in the dust. If I pushed through the miles, I could outrun the heaviness that settled in my chest after Teddy died.

But grief doesn't give a shit about race plans. It doesn't respect training cycles or taper weeks. It doesn't care how badly I want to feel okay.

There have been times when I've felt the familiar rhythm of my footsteps, my breath evening out, my mind clearing—where running really has felt like therapy. A release. A lifeline. But just as often, there have been runs where grief has hit me mid-stride, stealing the air from my lungs, buckling my knees, leaving me crying on a sidewalk while strangers drove past.

Some people run to escape.

I started running thinking I could do the same. That the further I went, the smaller my pain would become, stretched thin over the miles. But running doesn't erase grief. It just gives it a place to sit beside me.

And still, I run.

Because even when it hurts, even when the miles feel impossibly long, even when I'm dragging myself forward, step by stubborn donkey step, I know I can keep going. That I have kept going.

That's what running has given me—not freedom from grief, but proof that I can carry it. That I can lace up, show up, and do hard things. That even on the days when I feel weak, I am stronger than I think.

And running has given me something else I never expected: people.

Some of the best people I know, I met through running. Runners who, like me, carry loss and trauma and mental health struggles with them on every mile. People who understand what it means to run not for a finish time, but for our own well-being and for the people we've lost. People who know that some races are less about the clock and more about getting across the damn finish line, in whatever way we can.

I think about the people I've met through Team AFSP—the ones who lace up their shoes and take on miles for their lost loved ones. The ones who know that the weight of grief doesn't get lighter, but that we can build the muscles to carry it. The ones who remind me that grief doesn't have to be lonely.

I think about the messages I get from people who say, "I started running after losing my brother," or "I ran my first race in honor of my dad." These words hit me hard because I know what it means to take grief and turn it into movement, to let love and loss propel you forward instead of sinking you.

And I think about Teddy.

I don't know if he'd be surprised that I became a runner or if he'd laugh at the absurdity of it all. Maybe both. I know he'd be the loudest person at every finish line, embarrassing me with his cheering, and making brotherly jokes about how I made the ground crack by running on it.

And maybe that's why I keep running. Because in some small way, he's still here, with me, mile after mile.

Running didn't fix me. It didn't save me. But it gave me a way to live in the time after. And for as long as my body allows, I will keep running for myself. For the people I've met along the way.

And always, for Teddy.

Because, as my friend Guadalupe wrote ... WE run.

6

Every tattoo tells a story

Coming from a traditional Sicilian family meant never disobeying the rules, no matter how much we wanted to. The rules were clear, and the consequences even clearer. And yet, in the early 1990s, I broke one of the biggest: I got a tattoo.

My parents (and grandparents) had always said that if I got a tattoo, they'd kick me out. And I was not the kid who broke the rules. Ever. I was the responsible one, the one who worked hard, followed expectations, and did everything in my power to avoid disappointing anyone. But I had also spent my life forcing myself into the boxes other people had created for me. And I was tired of it.

So, when my college roommate Kristin and I walked into a tattoo shop that night, it wasn't just about rebellion. It was about proving to myself that I was my own damn person. I didn't labor over the decision or spend hours crafting a design that meant something. I chose a flash piece off the wall and chose the most improper place I could imagine: my left hip, right above my giant ass. (In my defense, that placement hadn't earned the label of "tramp stamp" back when I got that first tattoo ... I'm a pioneer; what can I say?!

And let me tell you, it wasn't some dramatic, movie-worthy moment where I clutched Kristin's hand in pain. It burned a little, but it wasn't awful. No tears. No gasping. Just me, doing something for myself. And that felt bigger than any pain ever could.

We walked out of that shop with fresh ink and adrenaline, convinced we were total badasses. That feeling lasted all of an hour—until we got to a local bar and had our coats stolen. And with them, Kristin's car keys. Suddenly, our rebellious night ended with us shivering outside in the rain, waiting for her dad to pick us up. Nothing humbles you faster than sitting outside a bar, broke, coatless, and freshly tattooed while waiting for a disappointed parent to rescue your dumb ass.

But I loved, and still love, that tattoo. Not for the design—it was just a random pick—but for what it symbolized. It was proof that, for once, I had done something entirely for myself.

And then, for years, I didn't do it again.

Not because I didn't want to.

Because I had made a promise.

During our Catholic pre-marital program, James told me he hated tattoos—and not in a passing, "I'm not really a fan" kind of way. Before we were even married, he asked me to promise that I wouldn't get another one. And without even thinking about it, I said yes.

I gave someone else permission over my own body without even realizing I had done it.

And I resented it.

Every single day.

It wasn't just about the tattoos, though that was part of it. It was the pattern, the way I had spent my whole life making myself smaller to fit into other people's expectations. The way I had quieted my wants, my own choices, to keep the peace. I loved the artistry of tattoos, their permanence, and the stories they could tell. But I had allowed someone else's preferences to dictate what I did with my own skin.

And then Teddy died.

The version of me that existed before his death shattered. And I had no interest in trying to glue myself back together in the way I had been before.

I didn't ask for permission. I didn't need anyone's approval. I told my family I was getting another tattoo.

It was Teddy's signature. A gift to myself. A reminder that no matter how much the world had shifted, no matter how much was lost, he was always with me.

And suddenly, all the rules, all the limits, all the careful ways I had tried to fit myself into other people's expectations felt pointless.

So I did what I had wanted to do for years.

I got another tattoo.

And then another.

And another.

Since then, each one has carried deep significance, far from the random design I picked off a wall. Every single one marks something important, tied to a moment, a milestone, or a piece of my story that I refuse to let fade.

My tattoos are not merely ink on skin; they are reminders, battle scars, tributes. A permanent way of saying this mattered.

I matter.

Some were born from grief, others from growth. Some are tied to joy, resilience, and reclaiming the parts of myself I had once quieted to fit into other people's expectations. But all of them, without exception, are mine.

And no one else gets a say.

*****

Tattoos have become one of the most visible ways I tell my story. Every piece of ink on my body holds a meaning, a moment, a memory that shaped me. Some of these tattoos were planned for months, and their designs were carefully chosen to honor love, loss, resilience, and transformation. Others were impulsive but no less significant—reminders that sometimes, the most powerful decisions are those made instantly.

Each tattoo is a part of me, but none exists in isolation. They are stitched together with the people who created them, the places where they were inked, and the emotions that made them necessary. Through tattoos, I am reclaiming my body as my own, writing my story on my skin in a language that can't be erased. And while every tattoo is mine, I didn't create them alone.

For years, I have trusted the artists at Pleasure in Pain Tattoo to bring my vision to life. One artist, in particular, has been a part of this journey. More than an artist, Paul Endres, Jr., is a true storyteller, helping to translate my grief, triumphs, and healing into something permanent.

The joke in our house is that while many families have a "family priest" (we have a couple!), our family also has a family tattoo artist. Paul has done many of my tattoos, some for my older kids and several cousins!

About Paul Endres, Jr.

Paul Endres, Jr, received his Master's Degree in Fine Art from the School of the Museum of Fine Arts, in Boston, MA. Since then, he has worked as a professional artist, painting and exhibiting his paintings in many galleries and national collections. Paul has received multiple awards for his work, and in 2019, a self-portrait painting of his was featured in the Academy Award-nominated film "Knives Out." Paul has taught many art courses, including 2-D Visual Design at Providence College.

In 2020, Paul made his longtime interest in tattooing his priority, and it has since become his primary medium. He creates tattoos in a variety of styles that often emphasize color.

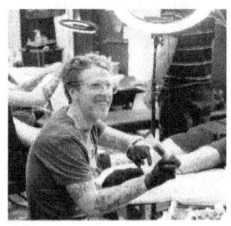

******

Teddy's Signature with Three Birds

March 1, 2020

Teddy remembered every holiday or event and always sent a card with a funny name listed as the return address, always with his distinctive signature. I found some of those cards while cleaning a box in our home office. Now I can carry them with me everywhere.

I've also incorporated three birds, each representing one of my kids, Jimmy, Abby, and Joey. They're the most important people in my life and always will be.

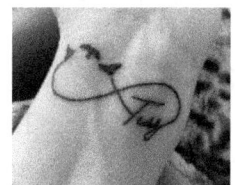

*****

Tree of Life Growing from a Book, Surrounded by Magic

Content Warning: Discussion of Non-Suicidal Self-Injury

The following section discusses non-suicidal self-injury (NSSI), also known as self-harm, including personal experiences with cutting. While this is not a discussion of suicide, it does explore complex topics related to mental health, trauma, and coping mechanisms.

I never wrote a post when I got this tattoo. At the time, it felt deeply personal, something just for me. It wasn't about making a statement or sharing a milestone. It was about reclaiming something I had lost.

Losing 50 of the 100 pounds I gained after Teddy's death was a victory, but the tattoo wasn't about the weight itself. It was about what it represented: healing. Movement. Growth. A conscious decision to take care of myself again after years of neglect. Years of saying that I did not matter in my brother's absence. Years of not living.

The design was intentional—a Tree of Life growing from the open pages of a book with sprinkles of magic swirling around its leaves. The placement was deliberate, too. It covers scars that have lived on my body for decades, remnants of an unhealthy coping mechanism I developed when I was ten years old: NSSI or cutting.

For those unfamiliar, NSSI is not the same as a suicide attempt. It's not about wanting to die—it's about wanting to feel something else. It's a way to regulate overwhelming emotions, to externalize pain that feels impossible to process. For me and so many others, it was a form of control when everything else felt out of control.

It didn't start as a big, dramatic thing. It was small at first, a release valve for emotions I didn't have the tools to manage. And then it became a habit. A secret. A fallback when the world felt too loud or too heavy.

No one in my life knew that I actively cut my flesh—or burned myself, or yanked out my hair, or even sometimes hit myself—when feelings became too overpowering, and I lacked the skills to process them. No one. Not my family or even my best friends. Something like that is easy to hide with clothing and an off-hand explanation. At least I told myself that.

That unhealthy coping mechanism didn't disappear when I got older. It followed me into adulthood, always lingering in the background, always an option. And after Teddy died, it became a favorite—an old, familiar escape in a suddenly unbearable world. It was easier, in some ways, to hurt myself physically than to sit with the weight of my grief. The pain was something I could see, something I could touch, something that felt real when everything else felt impossible.

But I wanted something different; I needed something different. So, I asked the artist to tattoo over the scars, effectively removing my access to that ugly area and also covering it with something beautiful.

I chose a tree because, like grief, healing isn't linear. It twists, bends, and reaches for the sun ... All while still deeply rooted in the past. The tree represents survival, resilience, and strength, not the kind that erases pain but the kind that continues to grow despite it.

And the book? That was never a question.

I have always found solace in words, in stories that felt like home. But no book ever meant as much to me as *A Tree Grows in Brooklyn* by Betty Smith.

I was in middle school, buried under the weight of loneliness, anxiety, and the too-big feelings that I didn't know how to manage. My mom, a teacher, came home one day with a book a student had thrown away—a battered old copy, its spine held together with duct tape, pages dog-eared and musty.

By all accounts, it was trash.

But to me, it was a lifeline.

Francie Nolan, the book's protagonist, was a dreamer—a girl who saw the world in stories. She survived by retreating into books and believing in the magic of words. She was scrappy, determined, hopeful, and heartbroken all at once. I saw so much of myself in her.

That book gave me something I desperately needed: the knowledge that I wasn't alone. That someone else, even if she was fictional, had felt like me and still managed to grow. Years later, as I sat in the tattoo chair, I thought about that beaten and worn book (which I still have and count among my most treasured possessions). I thought about how the words had saved me.

This tattoo wasn't just a celebration of weight loss. It wasn't just a way to cover scars and remove access to my favorite place to self-harm. It was a reclamation of my body. A quiet, permanent reminder that even in the darkest of times, I have always found a way to keep growing.

*****

Evil Eye "Family Tattoo" with Jimmy and Abby by Paul Endres, Jr.

June 1, 2021

Growing up, I wore a red ribbon pinned to my underclothes, had a gold *mano cornuto* and *cornicello*, and avoided eye contact with certain people ... All to protect from *il malocchio*, the Evil Eye.

Yet, no talisman was strong enough to protect against the all-consuming anguish of surviving Teddy's death by suicide, tormented by lingering questions, survivor's guilt, and obliterating pain. Jimmy, Abby, and I have scheduled a "family tattoo" of the Eye—a permanent amulet of protection.

May my children never again suffer a loss like that or feel a despair so deep that they can't reach out for my help. (Despite the laws banning tattooing minors in Massachusetts, ten-year-old Joey is lobbying to get a tattoo with us.)

*****

Blue Lobster

October 16, 2021

Nothing says I care about my health like wearing my Boston Marathon jacket while eating mini Charleston Chews ... I just celebrated running 26.2 miles with tattoo number five. This time, a lobster, symbolic of transformation and growth (among other things, like a stubborn nature... Maybe me, who knows?).

After three hours of tattooing, I felt a little dizzy and got myself a chocolate sugar rush. The box says this is three servings. I don't know what three people are splitting this one, but I'll take the 390 calories and eat the damn chocolate.

This tattoo was worth the wait, and it's difficult for me to be patient.

Aside from my general obsession with lobster and everything ocean, some things the lobster represents, or maybe some things that I seek:

- **Strength** - Lobsters become defensive when provoked and have a strong and stubborn character.
- **Protection** - One of the toughest shelled crustaceans, the lobster symbolizes resilience and a thick outward persona.
- **Regeneration/Transformation** - Lobsters can regrow claws and legs and molt throughout their lives, symbolic of continual growth and energy resetting.
- **Resolution** - Despite their more diminutive stature, lobsters go their own way and don't shy away from a fight with a larger predator.

I got the tough shell and stubborn character down ... But, why blue? Because a blue lobster is rare, and I never want to be considered ordinary.

*****

Sicilian Donkey by Paul Endres, Jr.

March 24, 2022

Just finished up a self-portrait tattoo, and I love her so much!

I've shared this Teddy story before, but it always makes me laugh. When we were little, the internet didn't exist. During those dark ages, we amused ourselves by looking up creative insult words in the dictionary. Of course, Teddy looked up "Jenny" and then died laughing when he read one of the definitions.

jen·ny | \ ˈje-nē \ (noun) A female donkey

Teddy took it one step further. He taught the adorable toddler twins next door to yell "hee-haw" whenever I walked by. At the time, I was not amused, even though I shared many qualities with the donkey.

Today, I trust that Sicilian donkey-ness will get me through, especially during the long races.

My therapist asked me what would happen if I used that same tenacity to show myself some compassion or (gasp) self-acceptance. My automatic response: Ummmmmm, no thank you. Of course, she challenged me to show myself some kindness each day and talk to myself the way I would encourage my own kids.

I've struggled with negative self-talk for most of my lifetime. And, like a donkey, I'm wicked stubborn (to throw in the Boston slang); so this will be a difficult task. But I'll try. No promises. Because, you know, hee-haw.

*****

Seahorse

May 7, 2022

I don't look like a runner. I'm not lithe, and I don't have six-pack abdominal muscles. I am heavy on my feet, and I'll never qualify for the Boston Marathon.

Yet ...

I am strong.

I am tenacious

Quitting is never an option, no matter how tough a course gets.

After the 2021 Boston Marathon, I got my favorite blue lobster with artist Dana Morse. It reminds me that I am resilient, strong, and capable of anything I set out to do.

I made the appointment for my newest tattoo the same day because I hoped to run again with Team AFSP at the 2022 Boston Marathon—just six months after the 2021 race!

It wasn't pretty or fast, but I completed one of the world's most difficult marathons—all 26.2 miles—twice in six months.

Meet my new lovely. I've named this beautiful and vibrant seahorse Stormy.

Aside from my general obsession with everything ocean and the fact that the female seahorse is the more assertive of the species, some things the seahorse represents include:

- **Strength** - In turbulent waters, the tenacious seahorse will hang on to something with its tail and never let go.
- **Vulnerability** - The seahorse is still quite vulnerable despite its tough exoskeleton. Recognizing your vulnerabilities is a way to empower yourself and grow.
- **Opportunity** - The beautiful seahorse, with its curly tail and changing colors, resembles a horse and a sea creature and is often a symbol of good luck and opportunity.
- **Authenticity** - As a spirit animal, the seahorse speaks to our ability to help others feel comfortable in our company. It is a symbol of charm without superficiality. I read somewhere, "Like a brilliant aquamarine, the seahorse's charm is genuine."

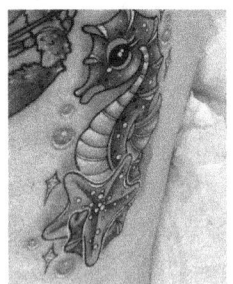

*****

Blue Jay

January 4, 2023

Whenever I see a blue jay in my yard, I think of Teddy. Blue jays are playful, and their calls remind me of Teddy's giggle.

I later read, "Some believe them to symbolize a connection with death, offering guidance as people pass on to the afterlife. Chinook culture identifies blue jays as benevolent tricksters that are protective towards humans, but with comical and somewhat foolish traits." (Birdfact.com)

Well, if that isn't Teddy!

I considered placing tattoo number eight on my forearm to see it when runs get tough and during races, during which I always save the last mile for Teddy. Then an online running friend (who, of course, I hope to meet in real life) suggested the opposite leg as the Sicilian donkey done by Paul Endres, Jr., so that as I run, I take one step for me and one for Teddy—like we were back together, racing to Grandma and Papa's house.

Thinking of that, I started to cry at the tattoo parlor. I don't cry a lot daily, so why not cry in front of a bunch of relative strangers? I'm pretty sure Teddy was laughing at me.

I plan to take it leisurely tomorrow morning and see how it feels in the evening. I don't want to lose my run streak, but I don't want to bleed out the ink. This is just too beautiful!

*****

Jellyfish by Paul Endres, Jr.

July 6, 2023

After each significant race I've finished in memory of my brother, I've gotten a tattoo. Today, I added a beautiful jellyfish to my menagerie of sea creatures.

Each tattoo is given a lot of thought, and this one is no different. Some symbolism or meaning includes tenacity and transformation amid turbulence or trauma.

And Joey was stung by one this Christmas. But once he felt better, he jumped back into the ocean like a badass. It's a good memory, for sure.

*****

Sagittarius Archer with Sister-Friend Kris in New York City

December 8, 2023

If nothing else, a Sagittarius is impulsive. Put two of them together, and it equals an epic day.

After my solo breakfast, I went ice skating for the first time in twenty years at Bryant Park.

Then, Kris and I did all the touristy things—the Saks clock, the Rockefeller Plaza tree ... And I brought my veteran New Yorker friend to a place she'd never visited, Top of the Rock. We even tried out the new Beam Experience, met a lovely couple (Jo and Nick) from the United Kingdom, and had "Happy Birthday" sung to us while we were dangling above Rockefeller Plaza.

We hopped on the subway and headed to the uber-chic Bang Bang Tattoo to get matching Sagittarius tattoos. Ironically, our new ink is so lovely and delicate, considering we're two Sicilians from Boston.

I'm so grateful to have a lifetime friend who lets me be me and laughs at the same stuff that made us giggle in Downtown Crossing Filene's in 1987. Heading home tomorrow, content and at peace.

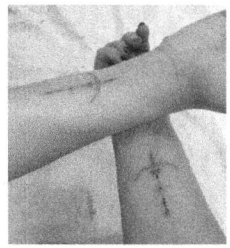

*****

"Enough" Tattoo with Running Friends in Virginia Beach

March 15, 2024

"Enough" doesn't need any additional explanation.

Thank you, Ethan, for the beautiful work ... and for saying I seem too nice to be from Boston. I'm not, but hey!

I told my mom, Mary-Grace, that I was getting her face on my ass, so this might be a letdown for her, but it's a reminder I need often.

*****

Flaming Phoenix Feather by Paul Endres, Jr.

April 16, 2025

Earlier today, I saw a meme that read, "Sometimes a princess, sometimes a terror," and I corrected it to read, "Never a princess, always a terror." A friend shared another correction underneath: "Don't fashion me a maiden that needs saving from a dragon. I am the dragon, and I will eat you whole."

Ironic, considering I was on my way to get tattoo number twelve.

And, just like me, it's no dainty symbol of strength. A feather, but not a soft, downy thing. This one burns, quite literally.

A fiery, burning phoenix feather that's everything I daydreamed it would be and then some. It says, "I've been through some shit and I'm still standing."

People love the phoenix metaphor—rising from the ashes, rebirth, resilience—all that resonates. But what we don't talk about enough is just how excruciating it is to burn. To lose everything familiar. To scream into silence and still wake up the next day, scorched and gasping, but alive.

That my phoenix feather is burning is intentional. It's about more than surviving the fire and rising from the ashes ... It's about continuing, even when everything is burning.

Its placement next to my Sagittarius bow and arrow is intentional, too. Another reminder of who the fuck I am. I'm still becoming. And I'm allowed to carry both the flames and the flight.

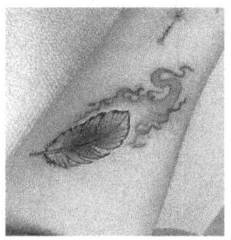

*****

I didn't grow up planning out future tattoos or daydreaming about designs. But life has a way of shifting our perspective and marking us whether we like it or not. Some scars we choose, some we don't.

My tattoos? They are the ones I chose.

Each carries a weight, a memory, a moment frozen in time. Teddy's signature is a permanent reminder of the brother I lost. The Tree of Life covers the scars of an unhealthy coping mechanism with something that represents resilience and growth. The Blue Jay, a little trickster forever in motion, just like him. The Sicilian donkey, because I am stubborn as hell if nothing else.

There's something about the ritual of it all—the moment I sit in the chair, the buzz of the needle, the pain that fades into something else. It's a process, a transformation, and in many ways, a reclamation. Every time I add something new, I write another chapter, reinforcing another truth: I am still here. I am still standing. I am still me.

But what I love most isn't just the tattoos themselves. It's the stories they tell—not just to me but to the people I meet along the way. Strangers stop me in the grocery store to ask about my blue jay. A fellow runner at the starting line points to my Evil Eye tattoo and tells me about her grandmother's talismans. A woman at a coffee shop spots my "Enough" tattoo and quietly says, "I needed to see that today."

These moments remind me why I keep adding to this collection. My tattoos aren't just mine. They're part of a conversation about grief, healing, and finding your way forward. They connect me to people in ways I never expected. And sometimes, they even serve as a reminder on the days when I need it most.

And, in case you haven't guessed ... I'm not done yet.

There will always be more stories to tell, more moments to mark. At the time of this writing, I've already sent an inquiry for my next piece—a flaming phoenix feather. Because if my tattoos say anything about me, it's that I refuse to stay down. That even in the hardest seasons, I will rise, again and again.

So, if you ever see me at a race, in line at the store, or sitting in a tattoo chair for hours, know—there's a story behind every line. And I will never stop telling them because some stories deserve to live on forever.

7

Laughing My Way Through Life

My laugh is loud. Not just a little loud. Not just oh, I didn't expect that from you loud. No, it's heads-turning-in-public, people-asking-me-to-keep-it-down, making-entire-rooms-stop loud. It's the kind of laugh that comes straight from the gut, unfiltered, and completely unbothered by social norms.

And I apologize for it. Constantly.

"Sorry, I know I'm loud."

"I'll try to keep it down."

"I know, I know—inside voice."

But my real friends? The ones who know me and love me for the unpolished, chaotic mess I am? They shut that apology down quickly.

"Stop apologizing for being happy, Jen."

"Never dim your joy just because other people can't handle it."

"You laugh with your whole body, and I love that about you."

And they're right.

I've spent my whole life trying to make myself smaller. Quieter. More digestible for the world around me. But my laugh? That's one thing I've never been able to shrink. It's as much a part of me as my sarcasm, stubbornness, or tendency to melt at random dog and raccoon videos.

Because here's the truth: I laugh with my entire being. I laugh with the same intensity that I feel everything else, with zero moderation and no concept of control.

People love to say, "If you don't laugh, you'll cry." I prefer to do both. At the same time, sometimes. Because, and this is the fucking truth, life is a lot. And sometimes the only way to survive it is to find something, anything, to laugh about, even when (especially when) nothing feels funny.

I grew up in a Sicilian family where humor was a love language and survival skill. We didn't do soft, delicate laughter. We did loud, boisterous, obnoxious belly laughing. It was roast or be roasted, and if you weren't quick on your feet, you would get verbally destroyed at Sunday dinner, most often by Grandma Jennie.

Of course, Teddy was the undisputed king of this. His humor was wild, inappropriate, and perfectly timed. He had the uncanny ability to make me laugh at the absolute worst possible moments.

When he died, I lost more than just my brother. I lost the person who always knew exactly how to make me laugh, the one who could turn the darkest moments into something ridiculous, the one who understood that humor wasn't about ignoring the hard stuff but about surviving it.

For a while, I wasn't sure if I would ever laugh like that again. Grief does that. It steals joy. It makes you feel guilty for feeling anything other than unbearable sadness.

But humor, like grief, has a way of sneaking up on you.

I remember standing at the luncheon with my best friend Jenn following Teddy's graveside service ... Numb, exhausted, and barely functioning. Mom's friends told us about how I came to them with a dirty diaper when the boys, Teddy and their sons, were infants. I was the oldest of the friend-cousins, with Meredith just a few months my junior. As I learned that I was told, "Change your own frigging diaper," AND that Meredith and I did just that, both Jenn and I burst into the most ridiculous, snorting laughter. We laughed until I had to sit down, breathless.

And just like that, I knew I was going to be okay. Not right away, not perfectly, but eventually. Because laughter is how I survive—it always has been.

Some people cope by meditating, doing yoga, or taking long, introspective walks on the beach. I make wildly inappropriate jokes at deeply inappropriate times, and honestly, it works for me.

I've had therapists try to tell me that humor is a defense mechanism, a way to avoid dealing with my emotions. And sure, for some people, maybe it is. But for me? It's not always avoidance—it's often also acknowledgment.

It's looking the worst moments of my life straight in the face and saying, "Okay, well, if I can't change this, I might as well make it funny."

Dark humor exists for a reason. It's not because people who've been through trauma are heartless—it's because we've felt things so deeply that sometimes, the only way to carry it is to laugh at the absurdity of it all.

For example, when I ran my second Boston Marathon, someone said, "Wow, I could never do that." And without missing a beat, I responded, "Yeah, well, my brother died, so my tolerance for suffering is pretty high."

Their face? Horrified.

Me? Laughing, because it was true.

People don't always know what to do with that kind of humor. And that's fine. My jokes aren't for everyone. But they are for me. And for the people who love me, who get me.

I used to apologize for my laugh. For taking up space. For making people uncomfortable with how loud or unfiltered I am.

But I don't anymore.

Because my laugh? It's one of the best things about me.

It's big. It's all-consuming. It's the sound of survival. Refusing to let life, grief, or other people's expectations shrink me.

So, if my laugh bothers you? That's a you problem.

Because I'm going to keep laughing. Loudly. Unapologetically. And if it makes people turn their heads in public? Good.

I hope Teddy hears it.

*****

Life is absurd. Some of the things I've written about in my morning posts? Even more absurd. These posts don't follow a neat, tidy theme, nor does my humor. It's chaotic, unexpected, and sometimes unhinged.

But every post, every ridiculous story, every weird and random thing that made me laugh—it's all part of what keeps me going.

So, here they are ... A random collection of moments that just made life feel a little lighter for a little while. There's no rhyme or reason to them, but they made me laugh.

I hope they make you laugh, too.

*****

December 14, 2013

The other day, there was (for the first time) a card from "Your trash men Matt and George." We usually don't give a gift to the trash men, but I thought that was nice, so I got Matt and George Dunkin gift cards. I addressed them, put them in a card, and wondered aloud how I would give them since I never see them.

At this point, Jimmy Hoye threw himself on the floor and spent a bit rolling around laughing. In between his giggles, he uttered: "Uncle Teddy and I played a joke on you!"

I called Uncle Teddy, who was laughing so hard he couldn't speak.

A Sicilian never forgets, boys. Mwahahaha ... Jerks.

*****

June 12, 2016

It was a nice visit with Grandma Jennie, Mom and Dad, Teddy, Aunts, and Uncle Bud. From the amount of food on the table, you'd think we were expecting twenty more people.

Uncle Teddy helped Joey make a paper airplane ... That Joey drew a picture of a butt and wrote "Butt" on. Can't spell his name. But can spell butt.

Thanks, Teddy.

*****

May 11, 2017

A dear friend said she'd always considered Teddy my reminder not to be so serious and to laugh more. She's right. And I always wished I could have even an ounce of his humor. Even now, as I try to process this horrific tragedy, I remember times he made me laugh. I cherish those memories and encourage Joey to keep his Uncle Teddy-ness.

*****

March 30, 2022

NINETEEN DAYS TIL THE BOSTON MARATHON!! I'd say cue me running in circles screaming, but it's a rest day.

Thought for the day: Hoop earrings are magical.

Where's the lie?

Today is packed. I've got a lot of meetings, some unexpected things added with a tight deadline, Joey's soccer practice, packing for a really special trip, a pedicure appointment, and about eight hundred pounds of laundry to fold.

But, I've got HOOP EARRINGS.

In fact, I put on a bigger pair than I usually wear just to channel their badass energy. I might even bring them on my trip to give me some extra confidence.

Whatever you do today, do it with the tenacity of a Sicilian donkey in HOOP EARRINGS. We've got this.

You are more than enough, and you are perfect just as you are right this moment.

*****

February 13, 2024

I like to laugh in case you haven't noticed.

We know (actual science stuff) that laughter can alleviate anxiety, reduce stress, and just make life less life-y. The release of endorphins from laughing acts as a natural stress reliever, if even just for a moment. But sometimes, a moment is all we need.

Laughter is also an awesome coping mechanism. Think about all the mental health memes we send one another, poking fun at our daily dumpster fires and chaos.

But did you know that when we find humor in the face of adversity, we tap into our resilience and strength? (That damn word again, I know. It's growing on me.) To find humor in the face of massive shit storms is a testament to our strength and flexibility.

If you're DFC (down for chaos) like me, you'll find humor in every little thing ... the more absurd the better. But, if you're more "humor-typical," that might be watching a funny TikTok or Reel, scrolling through humorous memes, or spending time with people who always know how to make us laugh. (Joey is available for hire, by the way)

While obviously not a cure-all, laughter is a fantastic part of any mental health toolkit.

I hope you get some laughs today. Bonus points if you snort-laugh or almost pee your pants.

*****

September 30, 2024

I have been on fast forward all day and just couldn't juggle work, Joey chauffeur service, a dog vet visit, and catching up on everything to complete a proper run.

But, of all days, I NEEDED to get out. To requote the reel I've been saying on repeat for days ...

"Do you hear me? I'm cranky. I'm tired. I worked hard at school."

So I got out. I forgot the watch, but I've done the route so often that I know the mileage.

Today is the final day of Suicide Prevention Month, and so today's Healing Miles are dedicated to my brother, Teddy Fusco, Jr. of East Boston, Massachusetts, who died by suicide in May 2017. I've shared so much about who my brother was that you probably feel like you knew him, too.

What I wouldn't give to hear his tee-hee giggle after he'd done something amusing. Or to suffer through his nuclear hot and spicy chicken drumsticks once more. Or to get a random text from him that included just a picture, whose meaning would only be known to us.

But none of those things will happen. Not in the TIME AFTER.

Again, today is the final day of Suicide Prevention Month. Tomorrow begins in October, and all the related messages will disappear and be replaced by October's message.

Yet, for families like mine, and for those living with mental health challenges or who are in crisis, suicide prevention matters every single day of the year.

If you've followed the Healing Miles stories of our loved ones this month, I hope you take from them this ...

- You are not alone, even when it feels like you are.
- Checking in on someone could make all the difference.

- Hope is there, even when it's too dark to see.

*****

December 4, 2024

I have a new mug! It reads, "At least my trauma made me funny." It's funny because it's true.

Humor has always been my lifeline. When things feel impossible, absurd, or just plain hard, I lean into the ridiculous. Why? Because it softens the edges.

It makes the heavy a little lighter and unbearable more bearable. It doesn't erase the struggle, but it gives me room to breathe. The ridiculous is where I find relief.

A too-serious world needs moments that make you loud laugh (if you've heard mine, then you knowwwwwwww). It's not about ignoring the hard stuff—it's about holding it differently.

I don't think I could survive life without laughing at the mess. Whether over-the-top sarcasm, a poorly timed joke, or just a moment so ridiculous it feels unreal, those little bursts of humor keep me going.

I wouldn't want it any other way.

*****

December 22, 2024

Yesterday, I was on the go from 7 a.m. until the evening because it's THE week of all weeks for all moms everywhere.

Joey and I delivered cookies while we were out for his haircut. And, in the most Christmas week example ever ... As we pulled down a friend's street, I saw her driving toward me.

I passed the cookies to her through our open windows, and we spoke briefly.

Me: "Merry Christmas."

Her (dripping in sarcasm): "Oh, it's a great time to be alive."

Me: (insert donkey laugh, because YESSSSSSSSSSSS)

I texted her afterwards, "You just nailed the entire spirit of the season for moms everywhere."

Her response was unexpected (edited): "I just want to really thank you. [I] have so much to do (shopping isn't even close to done) and I was so overwhelmed ... You literally laughing as my ridiculousness has turned my day around. I am so grateful for you."

That melted my Grinchy heart.

This season is tough for so many for an infinite number of reasons. But moments like these—the messy, ridiculous, drive-by cookie hand-offs and the honest acknowledgment of all the feelings—carry us through. We're all overwhelmed, exhausted, and maybe just a little bit done, but a shared laugh or kind word can remind someone to keep going.

The holidays aren't perfect (despite what you see on social media), but they don't have to be. Little connections make all the difference.

*****

January 17, 2025

Last night I shared a poem I saw:

"You will be too raw for some.
You will be too loud,
too big, too fierce,
too quiet, too deep.
These are not your people."
~S.C. Lourie

My friend Lila wrote in the comments, "Psht, just wait until March, we gonna a have so much bigness you will be the small spoon."

This will be my second time joining Lila, Jessica, and Amanda for a running weekend—our second Shamrock Half Marathon, even!

I remember apologizing a lot (as I often do) that first trip. Was I laughing too loud? Was I being too weird? Too awkward? Too relaxed?

They just laughed and accepted me. And told me to STOP APOLOGIZING.

I made gravy and meatballs for our pre-race pasta dinner. It made my heart happy to cook for them. Another woman and her hysterically funny young son joined us for the dinner, too. Even though it was our first time meeting in real life, I felt instantly connected with her and her kindness.

I laughed so much that weekend, and so hard my sides hurt. Nothing was off limits, and we had several incredibly deep conversations... Along with many ridiculously hilarious ones.

When my flight home was suddenly cancelled, I remember thinking this was my punishment for being myself. I was lucky to have Amanda with me at the airport—she and I weathered our delays together.

Our ongoing chat is my favorite group chat of all time (I hate group chats usually!). It's a little bit of everything—life, coffee, work, running, happiness and tears, memes, reels, and boobs. Thank you, ladies, for sharing a seat at your table. Love you!

*****

If there's one thing I know for sure, laughter has saved me more times than I can count. It has been the thing that carried me through the worst of days, the glue that held me together when everything else was unraveling. It doesn't erase the hard stuff, but it makes it bearable. It doesn't take away the grief, but reminds me that joy still exists alongside it.

I used to think that humor had to be contained, that there was a time and place for laughter and a time and place for silence. That my loud, unfiltered, borderline obnoxious laugh was something to apologize for. But life is messy and unpredictable, and if I've learned anything, it's that waiting for the right moment to laugh means you'll be waiting forever because there is no perfect time. There is just now. And if something is funny, I'm going to laugh. Loudly. Without hesitation. Without apology.

Some people might call it a defense mechanism. And maybe sometimes it is. But it's also a lifeline. A way to say, I'm still here. I'm still standing. No matter how much it has tried to break me, I still find joy in this world.

Laughter doesn't mean I don't take life seriously. It means I refuse to let life crush me. It means I can hold space for both the heartache and the hilarity, the grief and the absurdity. It means I can acknowledge the weight of the things I've carried while still finding room to laugh at the ridiculousness of it all.

And I hope that never changes.

Because if there's one thing I want people to remember about me, beyond the miles I've run, the causes I've fought for, and the struggles I've endured, I want them to remember my laugh. That unmistakable, room-shaking, head-turning laugh that refuses to be contained.

Because that laugh? It means I made it. It means I'm still fighting. It means that, no matter what, I will always find a way to keep going.

So if you hear my laugh echoing across a room someday, know I'm okay. And if you're lucky, I might make you laugh, too.

8

Suicide Prevention and Mental Health Advocacy is My Whole Personality Now

Much like running and covering myself with tattoos, I didn't set out to make suicide prevention my entire personality.

But here we are.

And I'm okay with that.

Because if I can talk about mental health and suicide and make even one person feel less alone—if I can say Teddy's name and make sure his story didn't end the day he died—then I'll keep talking. Over and over and over again.

Advocacy started the way most things in my life do: with a big ass emotion and a whole lot of stubbornness.

I've shared much of this in the earlier chapters, but I'll keep sharing my story if it can help even one person feel seen and understood. So, skip this part if you're sick of hearing about it.

When my brother Teddy died by suicide on May 5, 2017, my family and my world shattered. There's no other way to describe it. It wasn't just grief—it was devastation, disorientation, a complete dismantling of everything I thought I knew. I didn't feel like a "survivor." I felt like I was trapped in that single, horrible moment, reliving it over and over again while life carried on without me.

I lost more than my brother that day.

I lost my parents in a way, too, because the grief of losing a child is something no parent ever truly recovers from. I lost friends who didn't know what to say, so they just said nothing and disappeared. I lost my health because I was so consumed by grief that I neglected my own body, my own needs, my own life.

By the time the third anniversary of his death rolled around in May of 2020, I was exhausted. I wasn't sleeping. I had gained 100 pounds. I felt stuck. I knew I needed something, some way to pull myself out of the grief spiral that was swallowing me whole.

And then, in the middle of a global pandemic, when everything felt uncertain and terrifying, I started walking. Which later transitioned to running, and now here we are.

Healing Miles was born in the crappiest part of many people's history—during the global COVID-19 pandemic of 2020. Much like some people turned to sourdough starter and puzzles, I turned to advocacy to help me survive the pandemic and lockdown.

It started in September of 2020, during Suicide Prevention Awareness Month. I had signed up for a Boston 5K for Suicide Prevention, something I had done in person in years past. But with the pandemic forcing everything into a virtual space, I wanted to do something more.

I decided that for the entire month, I would dedicate the first 5K of each day not just to Teddy, but to others lost to suicide. I shared the idea in an online suicide bereavement group, and within minutes, people started reaching out. They sent me names, photos, and stories of their loved ones. They asked me to carry those names with me.

I carried a different person with me every morning and then shared their story online. And suddenly, this thing that had started as something just for me became something bigger.

Healing Miles isn't just about miles. It's about remembrance. It's about making sure these names, these people, are not forgotten.

When I run, I don't just carry my own grief. I carry theirs. The names of people whose families miss them just as much as I miss Teddy. The names of people who should still be here.

In March of 2021, I participated in my first official AFSP event. I had already been doing the work on my own: talking about suicide prevention, running in honor of Teddy, sharing stories. But this was different. This was stepping into something bigger than myself.

That first event led me to Team AFSP. I became one of their charity runners, wearing my singlet with Teddy's name proudly displayed on racecourses nationwide. And when I tell you that people notice that shirt? I mean it. Runners, spectators, volunteers—people stop me to talk about it. They tell me about their own losses. They ask about the blue jay tattoo. They share their stories, sometimes with tears or a quiet "thank you."

This is why I do it.

Because people don't talk about suicide enough. Because we treat mental health struggles like they're shameful, something to whisper about in hushed tones. Because even after everything we know, the stigma is still there.

And that has to change.

I wanted to do more. So I did.

I joined the Massachusetts chapter board of AFSP and immediately became involved in advocacy, awareness events, and policy efforts. In January 2024, I became the Board Chair.

Which, if you know me, is both wildly unexpected and makes total sense.

Being Chair meant helping to lead a group of passionate, dedicated people, each with their own deeply personal "why." It meant showing up in every way possible: organizing events, amplifying voices, shaping policy, and ensuring mental health and suicide prevention stayed at the forefront of the conversation. It meant fighting—over and over—for better resources, stronger systems, and a world where fewer families have to endure the kind of loss that mine has.

But life took a sharp left turn as it tends to do.

What I didn't expect was having to step away from that role far sooner than planned. The decision was not easy, not neat, and definitely not part of the plan I'd created in my head. But sometimes, advocacy asks more of us than we can give. And sometimes, taking a step back is actually the bravest and healthiest thing we can do.

Even though I no longer hold a title, the work isn't over. It never was about the title, anyway.

I used to think that maybe if I ran enough miles, shared enough stories, and helped enough people, I'd reach some invisible finish line where the grief wouldn't hurt quite so much. But, as I've said many times, grief doesn't work like that.

There's no medal at the end. There is no moment where it all just stops hurting. There's just continuing—one conversation at a time, one hard day at a time, one Healing Mile at a time.

At first, I thought this work would be about Teddy. Keeping his name alive. Making sure his story didn't end the day he died. And in many ways, it is. But it's also about so much more. Because I'm not the only one carrying this grief, I'm not the only one fighting this fight.

Since stepping into this world, I've met the fiercest, kindest, most relentless people—loss survivors, attempt survivors, mental health pros, researchers, and volunteers who refuse to let silence win. The ones I've marched beside, laughed with, cried with. The ones who lace up their shoes and show up repeatedly because they know that even if we can't change the past, we can fight for someone else's future.

This chapter isn't about the miles. It's about them. The people who made this work matter. The ones who remind me every single day why I started. And why I'll never stop.

Because suicide prevention isn't just something I do, it's who I am.

*****

September 27, 2020

Today, I walk for another lost sibling, Lisa Musgrave's brother, Michael Athens, who died by suicide in 2011. And though nine years have passed, Lisa thinks of her brother daily. Sending Lisa love.

Yesterday's Samaritans 5K was a fantastic display of love and kindness. Thank you to all who donated, participated, or walked independently and sent me messages of support and comfort. You are all simply beautiful.

Once the miles have been walked, the recap montage video uploaded, and Suicide Prevention Month ends, there are still people feeling depressed, lonely, or in crisis. Families are still grieving the loss of their loved ones taken by suicide.

And so I will continue to walk—for Teddy, for others, for you and for my family—for as long as I can and for as many as I can. because you are never alone, as you all have shown me. Much love to you all.

*****

May 11, 2021

Thank you to Taunton, Massachusetts' Mayor Shaunna O'Connell and the Municipal Council for allowing me the opportunity to speak to you this evening about normalizing conversations around mental health, the importance of suicide prevention initiatives beginning at the elementary level, Healing Miles, and the AFSP Marathon in a Month event.

A special thank you to AFSP Massachusetts Executive Director, Jessica van der Stad, for making the trip to Taunton to share information about available resources and programs with our city leaders.

And thanks to my daughter Abigail for her support, photo taking, and ride to City Hall so I could walk home and sneak in a few extra miles.

Jessica joined me for the first mile home (I got to meet her adorable dog Abu), then I went home to finish the night with just under nine miles. With just a few days to go, I've got 42.94 miles to reach my goal of 300 miles walked!

*****

June 3, 2021

"You never really understand a person until you consider things from his point of view—until you climb into his skin and walk around in it." ~ Harper Lee (from *To Kill a Mockingbird*)

I walked over 305.01 miles during the Team AFSP Marathon in a Month, aiming to do just that. To give a voice to suicide loss survivors and to share their loved ones with the world. To hopefully reach even one person who feels isolated, ashamed, or overwhelmed. Because we are never alone, I see you.

Thank you to the families who entrusted their loved ones to me for Healing Miles remembrance walks. You have all made a difference and touched lives in ways seen and unseen. To the parents of the youngest for whom I've walked, thank you for allowing me to share your children's stories with elected officials to advocate for K-12 suicide prevention education and training for students, parents, educators, and staff!

Thank you to the incredible 194 supporters who donated an astounding $10,937 to support my participation in this event. Because of your generosity, I raised more money to help AFSP than any individual or team nationwide! Your donations account for 17% of the money raised during the event!

My parents and I cannot thank you all enough. Teddy's golden heart is seen in every one of you.

Watch the video at: https://www.youtube.com/watch?v=d1nkW-JEDyU0&feature=youtu.be

*****

June 28, 2021

Something absurd happened today. For just a moment, I thought I would text Teddy to tell him the story, but then I remembered. Between that and a day of adulting, I felt deflated when I got home, and I walked by the package on our porch a few times, wondering what the heck I had bought in my sleep this time.

My heart nearly burst open when I finally opened the box and found the Team AFSP Marathon in a Month medal and award.

THANK YOU to the amazingly generous donors who helped me achieve the top individual fundraising spot and raise awareness and support for AFSP's lifesaving work. YOU DID THIS, AND I APPRECIATE YOU ALL.

Last night, a family friend gave me a beautiful card thanking me for listening when she needed it. The card was an unnecessary, though appreciated, gesture and a reminder of Teddy's continuing impact on this world.

Teddy, you're one of the first people I think of each morning and who I think of most often during quiet moments. I will always miss you and wonder why I'm here while you're not, but I'm thankful to see your impish sense of humor, kindness, and even some of your frustrating qualities in my kids. I'll continue walking Healing Miles to share your and others' stories until we can end suicide.

*****

July 14, 2021

Thank you to all the family and friends (old and new!) who have given so much of your hearts to support me during Team AFSP's Marathon in a Month. Your love and support kept me going across 305 beautiful Healing Miles.

Together with my parents, I am grateful for the opportunity to continue sharing Teddy's kindness by running the 125th Boston Marathon with Team AFSP. To be able to run this race in a city that meant so much to Teddy fills my heart—and I know he will be running beside me each step of the way.

Throughout the next few months—and from Hopkinton to Boston—I hope to give a voice to other suicide loss survivors, raise awareness for the lifesaving work of AFSP, and help even one person reach out for help and feel less isolated.

*****

August 10, 2021

"When we establish human connections within the context of shared experience we create community wherever we go." ~ Gina Green-lee (from *Postcards and Pearls: Life Lessons from Solo Moments on the Road*)

The human connections I've made through Healing Miles have helped move me along my own grief journey. It's not a linear journey. Some days I move forward, some days I move backward, but always with me are those who have shared their stories and the memories of their loved ones lost to suicide.

◇Ricky Duran, runner-up on season seventeen of the television reality show "The Voice," is sharing his own story to help others find understanding and community amid a decidedly isolating personal experience—be it depression, mental illness, or suicide. Ricky is more than a suicide prevention advocate. He is also a suicide loss survivor, as Ricky lost both his father and best friend to suicide.

Ricky partnered with AFSP to produce the song's music video. I'm incredibly thankful to Ricky Duran and the AFSP Massachusetts Chapter for the opportunity to participate in this impactful project and share my brother and my connection to this important cause.

*****

April 2, 2022, from Houston, Texas

Last night, I was up much later than my regular 7:30 p.m. bedtime, so my sixty-minute easy-pace run was slightly abbreviated so I could sleep a little longer.

Every moment of the AFSP 2022 Chapter Leadership Conference has been unforgettable. This morning, AFSP's Chief Medical Officer, Christine Moutier, shared this quote from Desmond Tutu: "HOPE is being able to see there is LIGHT despite all of the darkness."

I cannot think of another quote that could more accurately capture the vibe of this event. I'm among more than 300 individuals who have been impacted by suicide but who have hope for a world without suicide.

I've had the chance to connect with AFSP staff and volunteers from around the country, and while this is a positive experience, it is also incredibly emotional. Last night, a number of us talked about our losses—the trauma, guilt, and new purpose.

One woman, Carol from Ohio, told me that her brother Randy's heavenly birthday is today. We talked about sibling loss and our experiences. During my Healing Miles run this morning, I carried Randy and Carol in my heart.

*****

May 16, 2022

Thank you so much to the Taunton High School Our Minds Matter club for inviting me to speak with students about mental health, suicide prevention, and my grief journey.

There were so many incredibly thoughtful questions from this group of teens! I'm sure that some of the questions were difficult to ask, and I appreciate every single one. I hope my answers helped even one person feel less alone or better equipped to help someone they love.

I was particularly touched by the students who spoke with me following the presentation, including one teen who asked for a hug. I am holding space for all of you—you are not alone and can do hard things!

*****

May 23, 2023

I enjoyed running into Janet Anderson from the Taunton Education Association (TEA) at the gym today. The TEA is the union that represents the City's 550 educators and created the Support Our Students campaign.

If you're a parent of a school-aged child, it matters to you, your kids, their teachers, and school staff...

The goal of Support Our Students is to ensure that Taunton Public Schools has:

- Protocols that support our neediest students returning to the classroom and staying in school
- Staffing that supports expanded mental health services
- Alternative therapeutic learning environments that support all learners
- Community Collaboration that supports relationships between schools and families

I have attended community organization meetings with the TEA as a mental health advocate and as an AFSP Massachusetts Chapter board member. The teachers' union recognizing that mental health is health and impacts all our students, educators, and staff is not only important but also energizing.

It might be Mental Health Awareness Month, but our educators and students need support year-round.

*****

January 25, 2024, from Orlando, Florida

I haven't even been at the AFSP Chapter Leadership Conference for twelve hours, yet I've already learned so much.

I'm here not only as a volunteer and board member but also as the Massachusetts Chapter's new co-chair. I'll serve alongside the inspiring David O'Leary until the end of this fiscal year, when I'll take over as Chair. I'm grateful for this opportunity to serve and to learn from David.

I spent some time with Nicole, our Walk Chair from the Easton Out of the Darkness Walk. I enjoyed chatting with her in the lovely Florida sun.

Following the opening reception, I met two running friends for dinner at the Stubborn Mule. I picked it for the name and was delighted by all the donkey-themed artwork. I had so much fun connecting with them, and SO MANY LAUGHS.

If I wake up early, I'll run, but I'm setting a later alarm in case I can sleep in (until about 6:30!), considering I left my house at 4 a.m. today!

I look forward to a full day of learning and inspiration tomorrow.

*****

January 28, 2024

The AFSP 2024 Chapter Leadership Conference awards banquet is the (almost) culmination of several days filled with hope, healing, and ALL THE FEELS.

Over the last several days, I've had the opportunity to hear from AFSP about key goals for the coming year, learn from research and advocacy experts about what's working and where we still have work to do, and listen to some incredible and inspiring stories of loss, love, and hope.

I feel energized and excited about all of the possibilities we have to work together to stop suicide and bring hope to those affected by suicide.

Energized and excited are not words one would typically associate with suicide prevention. But there's no other way to describe this truly transformative experience.

I am grateful for AFSP and all they do and the bright lights I've met along this journey.

Congratulations to the AFSP Massachusetts chapter on winning Chapter of the Year—staff, board, partners, and especially the incredible volunteers who spread hope across the Bay State.

*****

February 9, 2024

I'm getting ready for the annual AFSP Massachusetts Chapter board meeting, which will be my first board meeting as co-chair. I am so grateful for this opportunity to serve alongside (and learn from) David O'Leary, help build the chapter, and bring more programs and resources to the Bay State, and further AFSP's mission to stop suicide and bring hope to those affected by suicide.

After our board meeting tomorrow, we'll attend a volunteer appreciation event. AFSP's work would not be possible without all of our amazing volunteers. I look forward to connecting with them and celebrating the hope they have shared with so many others.

As a board chair, one of my goals this year is to add volunteers, particularly those from underrepresented communities, professions, and age groups. "Suicide prevention for all" drives me.

For suicide loss survivors, this community and volunteering can help with healing. I know this firsthand.

*****

September 28, 2024

I am sitting on the roof deck of an Airbnb in Newburyport, Massachusetts, with two of my AFSP colleagues. We are tired and hungry, but our hearts are full.

Nearly 1,000 participants, volunteers, and community partners joined us today at Polar Park for the AFSP Central Massachusetts walk.

Every team, every individual, had a personal reason for being there. Some of us walked for someone we lost, some because we survived, and others because they were supporting someone living with mental illness.

Yes, there were tears—a lot of them. But there was also laughter, shared stories, and beautiful moments of joy. Because grief and joy don't cancel each other out, they can exist side by side. Today, we let ourselves feel both.

We walked for those we love and miss, and we hope that one day, we won't have to walk for this reason anymore. Until then, we keep showing up, step by step, carrying the memories and love in our hearts.

After some dinner and a cocktail, we'll all sleep early ahead of tomorrow's AFSP Massachusetts North Shore Out of the Darkness walk at Cashman Park. Hope to see you there.

*****

October 6, 2024

Thank you to the AFSP Massachusetts Easton Out of the Darkness walk committee and volunteers for making this special day possible.

I am so grateful to have attended as a participant, along with my family and Matt, another loss survivor whom I met virtually in an online running group and real life for the first time today!

I loved having my parents and my little family in one spot for the morning. It's not an "easy" day, but I hope we found comfort and healing during the event. I carried the names of many of my Healing Miles families' loved ones.

Auntie Jean was an absolute rockstar today. We didn't see the short route marked, and she walked almost three miles! Thank you SO MUCH for coming and sharing this special day with us. I love you.

It's worth pointing out that Daisy Buchanan did well today and enjoyed her first rides on a school bus.

Highlight reel of Daisy living her best life to come, but for now, I am already in my pajamas and might be asleep before dark.

*****

October 10, 2024

Sending an enormous debt of gratitude to the Vernon Hill American Legion Post 435 for their incredible support of the AFSP Massachusetts Chapter

Our veterans face unique challenges, both during and after their service. The suicide rate among veterans is one and a half times greater than that of the non-veteran population, and over 6,000 veterans die by suicide each year.

This is a national tragedy, and we must continue to make veteran suicide prevention a national priority.

Thank you again, Vernon Hill American Legion Post 435, for supporting this crucial work and all you have done and continue to do.

Together, we can save lives.

*****

January 18, 2025

Today, I have a volunteer commitment, one I am honored to attend and to table for AFSP.

The Kacie Project is hosting a free QPR training at Taunton City Hall. If you're unfamiliar with QPR, it stands for Question-Persuade-Refer and is the mental health equivalent of CPR.

Steve Palm is the founder of The Kacie Project, which he created following the suicide of his fourteen-year-old daughter, Kacie.

When Steve reached out to see if I was available, my answer was OF COURSE. Steve was one of the suicide loss survivors I met at the Kitchen Table Conversations offered through the Bristol County Coalition for Suicide Prevention. Since that time, I have come to know Steve better and am continually inspired by his advocacy work.

Today's QPR training is special because it is also Kacie's birthday. She should be celebrating twenty-five, but instead, she is forever fourteen.

Kacie Elizabeth Palm of East Taunton, MA, died by suicide in July 2014, just months before she was to begin high school. She loved her family and animals and was known for her big laugh and compassion for others. Kerry and Steve, I'm thinking of you and Cameron today and every day.

If you need a reminder that THIS WORLD NEEDS YOU, this is it.

You are loved.
You are enough.
You are not alone.

*****

February 1, 2025, from Houston, Texas

Dear Teddy,

I'm sitting in bed in a hotel in Houston (remember when we almost moved here?!), holding a plaque that reads, Chapter of the Year – Large Market. That's right ... The Massachusetts chapter of AFSP won this at the national leadership conference. Seven awards in total. And all I can think about is YOU.

This was never supposed to be my life. But then you died, and I had to figure out how to keep living.

So I ran. I wrote. I spoke. I fought. I found people who understood. And now, I help support programs that save lives. This award—belongs to every volunteer, every survivor, and everyone fighting to ensure fewer families know about this kind of loss.

But part of me wants to believe it belongs to you and me.

I'll never stop wishing things were different. That I was texting you something dumb or muttering, "Fuckin' Teddy," instead of writing this. But if I have to live in a world without you, I will make sure your name isn't just a statistic.

I miss you, Teddy. I hope you saw that moment when we won. And I hope, somehow, you're proud.

*****

March 6, 2025

I believe in showing up honestly, even when it's hard—especially when it's hard—because if sharing helps even one person, it'd be worth it.

On Sunday, I was not okay. The weight of the last several months broke me, and I started crying and didn't stop until yesterday. I'd been in survival mode, slipping into old rigidity and over-functioning patterns, trying to control what's uncontrollable. It's a trauma response, not a solution.

Sunday night, when everything felt impossible, I had a self-harm relapse to quiet the suicidal ideation that was so fucking loud. At that moment, I did what I told others to do in every post—I texted 988. Because I knew if I didn't, things would get worse.

That was when I knew I was doing too much.

On Monday, I made one of the most difficult decisions of my life: I resigned from the AFSP Massachusetts Board. I love this organization and this work, but I was stretched so thin that I wasn't leading. I was reacting. And I didn't like who I was becoming.

But this time, I didn't hide it. I told close friends instead of swallowing it down. I let them hold space for me when I couldn't hold it for myself.

Last night, my dad said, "I'm proud of you for recognizing that you needed to step down for your own physical and mental health." And I felt my shoulders drop just a little.

That doesn't mean I'm at peace with my decision. It doesn't mean it doesn't hurt. It doesn't mean I don't feel untethered.

I broke out in shingles. Again. My body keeps the score, and it's screaming at me to slow down.

So I'm listening. But I'm still here. I'm still an advocate. Healing Miles is not something I will ever quit. I will still volunteer with AFSP. I will still fight for suicide prevention. But I had to make this choice to keep fighting at all.

That's the truth of it. No neat bow. No happy ending. Just this.

*****

For all the ways I talk about suicide prevention, I know that words alone aren't enough. Awareness is essential, but real change—the kind that saves lives—takes more than just talking. It takes action. It takes showing up. It takes people willing to have the hard conversations, push for better policies, and refuse to let stigma keep winning.

And that's precisely what we're doing.

Over the years, I've seen how this work ripples outward. It's the parents who tell me that sharing Teddy's story helped them talk to their kids about mental health. It's in the people who approach me after an event, quietly admitting I lost someone too. It's the runners who see my Team AFSP shirt during a race and give me a knowing nod because they're running for someone, too. It's in the conversations that happen when no one else is watching—the moments when someone finds the courage to ask for help instead of suffering in silence.

This chapter isn't just about me. It's about the people who have stepped into this fight alongside me. The ones who know that suicide prevention isn't just a cause—it's a commitment. The AFSP volunteers work tirelessly to spread hope, and the loss survivors who turn their grief into action. The advocates who demand change, fight for resources, and won't accept thoughts and prayers as policy. The friends who show up again and again because they know how much this matters.

And it's about the people we're fighting for—the ones still here—the ones we refuse to lose.

This work doesn't end, not with a single event, or a single law, or a single mile. It's ongoing. It's relentless. And I'll keep going as long as there are lives to save, stories to share, and hope to give.

Because that's what this is really about. Not just remembering those we've lost but fighting like hell for those still here.

Please, keep fighting.

9

Healing Miles: A Path Paved with Remembrance

Some miles are just miles. Steps taken, distances covered, routes logged and forgotten.

And then there are the miles that mean something. The ones that carry names, stories, and the weight of love and loss. The ones that remind me that while grief may be personal, it is never solitary.

When I started Healing Miles in September 2020, it was just for me—a way to honor Teddy and keep moving through my own grief. But it instantly became something much bigger than myself and my emotions. Other loss survivors reached out, sharing their stories and their loved ones' names, asking me to carry them with me, which I did.

And I still do today.

Each name I've run or walked for is someone who should still be here. A life that mattered. A story that didn't deserve to end too soon.

These remembrances are not just social media posts. They are proof that love does not disappear when someone dies, that the people we've lost are still known, still spoken of, and still carried forward—one step, one name, one mile at a time.

Here are just a few of the lives I've had the honor of remembering through Healing Miles.

Their stories stand on their own. They always will.

*****

September 22, 2020

Brrrrrrrr, it was cold this morning. I'm trying to accept that these colder mornings mean slower walks. I don't know why, but we did it again. And Penelope is pleased that she got two "what a pretty dog" compliments today.

Today is dedicated to the memory of Bill Jordan, who "struggled every day to accept his gift of life." I also walk for his daughter, Rebecca, as she struggles with the complex trauma and grief of the suicide loss survivor. Rebecca, I am always here to talk.

As Bill battled conflicting emotions throughout his lifetime, it is not uncommon for suicide loss survivors to experience survivor's guilt. People coping with their loved one's suicide often get less support because it's hard for them to reach out, and because many others are not sure of what to say or how to help.

*****

October 2, 2020

There are many reasons to stay in bed this morning: I didn't sleep, my hip is on fire, and I have a headache. But I got up and got out. Penelope kept looking to see why I was moving so slowly, but I moved. And we finished. Because I'm stronger than the cramp in my hip and tougher than I thought I was.

I don't personally know most of the families for whom I walk, but I do know and hold dear some for a million different reasons. Theresa showed me kindness in a place far from kind, and I will never forget her for those moments. She recently reached out to ask me if I would consider walking in memory of her brother Derek, who died by suicide in January 2011.

When I responded that I would be honored to walk in Derek's memory and do so on October 2, Theresa's response took my breath away.

Today is Derek's birthday. This is one of those "winks" that make me believe that our loved ones are still here, reaching out.

Of her brother, Theresa shared the most beautiful sentiment: "Son, brother, godfather, husband, friend, writer, poet, painter, gardener, farmer. Derek was passionate about the spoken word, animals, nature, and children ... He was devoted to his wife, and his goddaughter was his world. Derek's heart was just too gentle, and he was tired from fighting his demons. Miss him with all my heart, but I'm at peace as I know his soul is finally free of pain."

Happy heavenly birthday, Derek. And, much love to you, T.

*****

November 3, 2020

This morning, snow gave way to sleet, rain, and bitter cold. I'm able to walk longer in the mornings this week because I took some time between jobs to reset and recharge, though my ability to just "chill" and be alone with my thoughts disappeared after my brother Teddy's suicide. I hope to try meditation, but my reflection time is limited to these daily Healing Miles walks.

Today, I walk for Dreak Scott of Tyler, Texas, who died by suicide in August 2020. His mom, Toni Seaton, shared, "I miss his smile, his FaceTime calls, I miss how he acted as though he was my parent and not the other way around. He was always so encouraging and uplifting... No matter what he was going through, he was a poet and one of the most encouraging people you would ever meet." Dreak was a personal trainer at the Tyler Athletic and Swim club, where he was known to tell his clients, 'Slow Boogie is better than no Boogie.' In other words, to be here working on yourself, making slow progress, is better than no progress."

The news of Dreak's death shook the entire Tyler community. Toni shared a clip from a local news story. In it, the Tyler Athletic and Swim

Club is quoted: "Dreak was a shining light in all of our lives, and we hope that his memory lives on in all of us and all of you who had the pleasure of knowing him."

I'm continually struck by descriptions of "a smile that lit up a room" or the countless remembrances of a gentle soul who seemed devoted to helping others. In the YouTube video shared by Dreak's mom, Toni, on the Tyler Athletic and Swim Club Facebook page, and on Dreak's memorial wall, I read this over and over: "Dreak left a great mark on the heart of everyone he met. He was a good man with one of the kindest hearts I have known."

Toni, sending love as you begin to navigate life without Dreak.

*****

December 27, 2020

Each of these lives lost to suicide profoundly affects me, though some are more difficult than others, if that's even possible. I lay awake much of last night thinking about a life not yet lived.

Today, I walk Healing Miles in memory of ten-year-old Sean Jamor Savage, Jr. of Montgomery, Alabama, who died by suicide on March 10, 2015, just six days shy of his eleventh birthday. This sweet baby loved animals and his family, taking things apart to rebuild them. He was intellectually gifted; Sean's IQ was incredibly high, and he attended a gifted student program and always maintained a personal business plan. Sean's mom, Tamie Lewis, shared, "I miss hearing my son's voice. I miss him calling me mama. I miss his smile ... I miss going into his room at night and kissing him on his big cheeks...He had the prettiest brown eyes."

Let this sink in. Sean was just ten years old.

Barely a preteen, still with a "baby" face and little boy voice. He'd be 16 today, preparing for a pivotal year in most teens' lives: a driver's license, college tours, prom, and more. Yet, Sean is forever ten.

His family has been irreparably changed. Tamie and her surviving children suffer from PTSD, and she shared that her children experience suicidal ideation, which is not uncommon for suicide loss survivors. Tamie feels that she missed signs of mental illness, and I imagine those what-ifs keep her awake at night. Yet, through her agonizing pain, Tamie hopes to form a nonprofit to support and uplift young kids like Sean who battle anxiety, depression, and mental illness. "Maybe through my pain I can help save somebody else's child."

*****

December 15, 2020

I considered "I think you should reconsider walking on the icy road tomorrow" a challenge. Because, well, I'm a stubborn Sicilian donkey. And because Penelope and I have missed our Healing Miles morning walks and the peace of the Taunton Green before dawn, we said "good morning" to Teddy as we passed his banner.

Today, I walk in memory of twenty-year-old Brandon "Apollo" Lanier of Salt Lake City, Utah, who died by suicide in June 2019. Brandon was born on his mom, Gaby Galeas's, nineteenth birthday. It is bittersweet now as Gaby will never again celebrate her birthday with the best gift she ever received. He was described as incredibly selfless, caring for family, friends, and even strangers. "My son was an amazing human who just wanted to be loved ... He was so funny, always telling jokes, and had a million-dollar smile." This photo of Brandon is the last he ever posted on social media, captioned "All smiles."

Gaby shared a list of life goals Brandon started, "47 Plans to Love Life." The incompleteness of this list strikes me, halted abruptly after 38, and with "Love myself" listed as his first plan.

One of Brandon's goals was to expand the "Love Sandwich" project. When Gaby asked her other children about this, she learned that Brandon wanted to make sandwiches to feed the hungry. In fact, on the day before he died, Brandon brought a stranger into a burger joint to buy him a meal. It was just the kind of thing he did.

To honor Brandon's memory and help raise suicide awareness, Gaby and her children brought the Love Sandwich project to life, feeding more than one hundred people in their community. The shirts, designed by Brandon's sister, capture his heart and smile. They hope to do this again on January 3 to celebrate Brandon's birthday and again as often as they can. What a beautiful way to honor this brief, beautiful life. Sending you love, Gaby.

*****

February 3, 2021

After twelve days off, Penelope and I chose a snowy morning for our first morning out in almost two weeks. We took it slow and carefully, mostly walking in the street—a much-needed walk with Penelope.

In September, I walked in memory of seventeen-year-old Kai Harvey of Staffordshire, United Kingdom, who died by suicide on February 3, 2020. Today, I walk to honor his first angelversary. In the Fall, his mother Lynette wrote, "My beautiful son ... so talented and unique." Over the last several months, I've learned that this gentle young man loved music (including Joy Division, a band whose songs are all over my playlists), his big, beautiful family, his friends, and making others laugh. At Christmas, his family put up a tree just for Kai, filled with ornaments sent from family and friends. It is such a beautiful tribute to a young man gone far too soon and a lovely way to mark a family's first season without their son and brother.

Today, the Harvey family remembers Kai amid the United Kingdom's COVID-19 lockdown. They'd planned a big get-together, but instead released balloons at 4:26 p.m. They asked family and friends to honor his memory in any way they wished—apart but together in their love for Kai. Lynette has become a friend, though we've never met. I brought a few Dunkin gift cards with me this morning and shared some smiles along our route in honor of Kai.

Lynette and family, sending you all love.

******

April 17, 2021

After yesterday's storm, this morning's sun was welcome.

Today, I walk in memory of Patrick Jinks of Panama City, Florida, who died by suicide on April 17, 2020, one year ago today. I first walked for Patrick in October 2020 at the request of his mom, Cindy. Back then, I shared what I learned from Cindy, "… Patrick had a smile and laugh as big as his larger-than-life personality. He was a selfless helper of all, 'the light in the dark.'"

Since then, I have gotten to know Cindy, and I think of her often. She lives with a grief that no parent should, and she continues with love to honor Patrick's memory. From a beautiful tattoo incorporating the ocean, which Patrick loved, to a bear made from his suit, to a lovely seaside bench at Patrick's favorite spot, Cindy keeps her beautiful son's memory alive.

Birthdays, holidays, missed milestones. They're painful reminders of our loved ones and what they've missed. But, anniversaries—angelversaries—are particularly difficult to navigate as a suicide loss survivor. They're often reminders of moments of panic, terror, and abject horror as the truth of the situation is realized. Cindy, I am sending you much love today and always.

*****

April 21, 2021
AFSP Marathon in a Month DAY 3
MILES walked: 41.95

It was 64° at 5:30 a.m. This was my first morning walk without a jacket this year. It was a beautiful morning walk with Penelope. After ten miles, I flopped in a chair, but she chased Gus at top speed.

Today, I walk Healing Miles in memory of Levi Watkins of Roachdale, Indiana, who died by suicide just over two months ago in February 2021. His wife Karla Watkins shared, "I miss Levi's laugh; it was contagious. He was always happy and full of life. Levi was an amazing husband and dad. Between the two of us, we had four children and two grandbabies. Levi was so creative and was always building something. Our home is filled with projects that Levi designed and built. He was an avid hunter and fisherman; he loved nature and being outdoors."

I first met Karla in the Fall of last year. On Halloween, following a surprise snowstorm, I walked in memory of her son, Kylar Galloway. My heart hurts for Karla and her family—so much loss in just a few short years. I carry you all in my heart, Karla.

*****

January 15, 2022, from New York, New York

11°F in New York City this morning, -2°F with the wind chill. I bundled up and made my way through Central Park with a destination in mind: Bethesda Terrace. At the fountain, I stopped my running watch and sent love to a childhood friend as he marked his sister's third angelversary and to Karla Watkins on the heavenly birthday of her son Kylar Galloway.

I first met Karla when I walked Healing Miles in memory of Kylar on Halloween 2020. Karla's life has been deeply impacted by suicide. We've gotten to know one another virtually, and her perspective and humor have helped me along my own grief journey. My dream is to complete a walk or run to raise awareness around suicide prevention and mental health in every state. Indiana is at the top of my list, so I can meet Karla and hug her enormously.

*****

March 22, 2022

I met with my running coach virtually last night. When we reviewed my plan for the week, I shared that it was important that I complete a strength training session today on the angelversary of Jim Puggi, a competitive bodybuilder. She agreed but stressed that I should keep it short and at a lower intensity.

This adjustment seems appropriate for Jim Puggi's remembrance. When I met his daughter, Morgan Glickstein, she shared that she often "witnessed him struggle to take breaks or skip gym days and even get injured." So, I put aside my need to always go all out for lighter weights and lower intensity to ensure my body is ready for the Boston Marathon in twenty-seven days!

Joey and I traveled to Philadelphia in October to support Morgan and Team Puggi at the AFSP Out of the Darkness walk. We'd never met, but Lisa and Morgan feel like family. I especially love the immediate bond between Joey and Lisa, who, like my brother Teddy, loves over-the-top pranks. Lisa even helped me play an epic prank on James during the 2021 Boston Marathon.

Sending love to Morgan, Jim's wife Lisa, and his family and friends today and every day.

P.S. (added June 2025) Morgan, choo choo! Love you!

*****

July 8, 2022, from the Alto Vista Chapel in Oranjestad, Aruba

I felt guilty about missing this morning's run until about twenty minutes into our island excursion. The day included swimming in a natural pool, walking, climbing ninety-nine rock stairs, and a full body workout along the ride, holding onto the truck's sides.

We visited many beautiful spots in Aruba, including the Alto Vista Chapel in Noord, the adjacent Peace Labyrinth, and hiking trails.

In the chapel, I lit one candle for Jack Griffin Rowland and one for Teddy, whose heavenly birthdays are today and Sunday. Outside the Peace Labyrinth, a kaleidoscope of colored ribbons reminded me of Destiny Pettry and her mom, Jennifer. As I walked the Peace Labyrinth, I thought with gratitude about each step I have traveled on this journey, particularly during the last year.

I'd brought with me two memory stones—one for Teddy and one for young Jacob Hughes. I wasn't sure where to place the rocks until a little blue lizard ran over my feet. Twice. Thanks for the hint, Teddy.

We did so much during that four-hour excursion that I fell asleep in the Jeep on the way back to the hotel. I dreamed of a Bald Eagle. Any ideas?

*****

September 10, 2022

Today is World Suicide Prevention Day.

Five years ago, my brother Teddy died by suicide. His death shattered our family and our world and thrust us into the worst club to which no one ever wanted membership.

My eighteen-mile run today was for Teddy. And for my Team AFSP sister-friend Vicki's Dad. And for so many others.

I completed my run as a virtual participant in the Sort'a Mountain Stage Race / Sam's Race. I learned of it through the organizer, Chris, a fellow runner and suicide loss survivor. Proceeds from the race support

Sam's Foundation (a suicide prevention charity), which Chris founded following the suicide of his son Sam.

The first fourteen miles went well. Mile fifteen was tricky, as the traffic was heavy, and I walked most of it. If mile fifteen was difficult, then sixteen and seventeen felt excruciating. I started having stomach cramps and chills around the middle of mile seventeen and was forced to call James to pick me up. I paused my watch, went home, got sick, and finished the final half mile for eighteen miles total. It was not my best time by far, but I felt accomplished.

Teddy, I know you're laughing your ass off right now.

*****

September 23, 2023

Six miles on cement legs after yesterday's eighteen miler. Quite the metaphor ... I had to dig deep and keep going when I wanted nothing more than to quit.

- According to the World Health Organization, nearly 700,000 people around the world die by suicide each year.
- And for each suicide, many more people attempt suicide.
- Across the globe, suicide is the 4th leading cause of death among all people aged 15-44.

Why aren't we talking about it more than just in September?

Today, the amazing Angie Comerford and friends are walking eleven miles up the coast in the United Kingdom to raise awareness for suicide prevention. They carry a banner similar to this with so many names of people lost to suicide, my brother among them (thank you, Angie!).

My gym permitted me to hang a banner on the treadmill as I ran in solidarity with Angie's Walk of HOPE today. Thank you, Work Out World!

Not surprisingly, only a handful of people asked about the banner and the names. Many more walked past and side-eyed it but didn't say a word.

Let's start talking about suicide and mental health the way we talk about physical health. Because in doing so, more people will feel empowered to reach out for help when in crisis. Together, we really and truly can stop suicide.

*****

September 29, 2023

My mental health has been in the toilet all week, so today's long run was needed. Since I've been sick and am immunocompromised (because I do not have a spleen; it was removed to address hereditary spherocytosis), I opted for the treadmill as we got another day of rain.

Today's Healing Miles are in memory of brothers Danny Martinez of Los Angeles, California, and Rudy Aguilar of Denver, Colorado, who died by suicide in February 2010 and January 2016, respectively.

Of Danny, sister Guadalupe shared, "He was smart, funny, he would take apart mom's alarm clock because he wanted to see how it worked.' He was charming, a true ladies' man." And of Rudy, she shared, "He loved sports, was an encyclopedia with all things about the Lakers, Kareem Abdul-Jabbar, and Magic Johnson. He knew all of the stats. When he was a kid, he would go to the local park, sign himself up for the sport of that season, and take it to mom to sign for permission."

"So many memories left untold, everyday simple moments," Guadalupe wrote. "I miss them every day, but I carry them with me as I raise them out of the darkness and into the light."

It's only fitting that my longest run in Suicide Prevention Month be dedicated to the brothers of one of the fiercest suicide prevention advocates I know. I first met Guadalupe in March 2022, running with Team AFSP at the Los Angeles Marathon Charity Challenge (half marathon).

I am continually amazed and inspired by the work that Guadalupe does to end the stigma around mental health and suicide, and I consider her one of my dearest friends.

I love you, Guadalupe!

*****

September 4, 2023

Today's Healing Miles are in memory of Eric Shepherd from Weatherford, Texas, who left us far too soon in August 2020.

Running on my rest day, I'm reminded of the strength and resilience that binds suicide loss survivors together. While I hate that we are part of this truly horrible club, I'm grateful for Terra Shepherd's unwavering support and friendship since I first walked for her husband, Eric, in September 2020.

That first walk for Eric was special—it was one of the very first Healing Miles remembrances I completed. Back then, I didn't anticipate how this grief journey would reshape my life in countless ways, big and small.

Terra misses Eric's laughter and smile more than anything. She once shared, "Eric had such an amazing soul; kids and animals loved him so much! He would give the shirt off his back to anyone. The world feels incomplete without him... He loved hard!"

I love you, girl. I remember Eric today and always.

*****

September 26, 2023

Today's Healing Miles are in memory of Katherine Thompson Diedrichsen of West Bridgewater, Massachusetts, who died by suicide in March 2012. Katherine is remembered for her devotion to her family, kindness, and sense of humor.

Her brother, Dave Thompson, shared a few things he misses about his sister: "Her infectious laugh and smile. Her love of her daughters ... I miss knowing that she was the glue that stayed connected with my parents and my brother ... I'm grateful for how much I've learned and grown because of her and how much I still do, but I miss that others didn't get to meet her and how much is lost and forever changed with her not here."

Dave also shared a few blogs that he wrote following Katherine's passing. He wrote that a friend, "Stacie added, 'I will always remember her one of a kind smile and laughter with an occasional snort mixed in for the really funny moments that life brought.'"

I first met Dave in June. He's part of AFSP Minnesota and chaired the Grandma's Marathon team. Dave gave me one of the single greatest gifts I've ever received: The gift of normalcy. We talked about our siblings, how our families changed, how we'd been affected, but in a way that felt natural—like he could see into my heart and me into his. We laughed about truly ridiculous things, too. Though we had a short time together, I will always carry it in my heart. Dave, you are one of my favorite people. You're beyond wicked awesome, and I totally will have a tattoo for you someday.

Dave, thank you for sharing your sister and for all your mental health and suicide prevention advocacy. Sending you love every day (and lots of hoochie short memes).

*****

December 1, 2023

Six low and slow miles to start December. My knee is still a little sore but getting better. I'm \looking forward to breaking in my new running shoes, which will undoubtedly help.

Received a message from my dear friend Carlos today. He lost his uncle, who was more like a brother, to suicide many years ago. Today is Jose Luis Ortiz's heavenly birthday, which is still difficult for Carlos. I carried Carlos and Jose in my heart throughout tonight's Healing Miles.

Many people have commented that they expected anniversaries, birthdays, and milestones to get easier over time. The reality for many is quite the opposite. No matter how well we prepare ourselves, the grief tsunami seems to engulf everything in our world.

There's no timeline on grief, no finish line. We learn to carry it a little differently, but it is always part of us. And that is normal. For what is grief if not love with no place to go?

*****

April 24, 2024

Twenty-seven years ago today, my friend Nicole lost her mother to suicide after a long battle with bipolar disorder. Nicole was seventeen years old—a high school junior—and at an age when many mothers and daughters are excitedly prom dress shopping together.

But, like many kids who grew up in a home clouded by mental illness, these mother-daughter moments were few for Nicole. In many ways, bipolar disorder robbed her of this special relationship long before suicide.

Today, Nicole is the mom of three beautiful and amazing daughters. When she talks about them, her whole face lights up. I love that for Nicole—while she didn't experience the joy of a healthy mother-daughter relationship as a child, she now pours her heart and soul into cultivating one with each of her girls.

Nicole, I am so grateful to have met you. You are a light in this world for so many, including me. Thank you for all you do to stop suicide. Keep fighting, you amazing warrior. Love you.

*****

May 14, 2024

Today's Healing Miles are in memory of Paul "P3" LaRochelle II of Auburn, Massachusetts, and Chicago, Illinois, who died by suicide in February 2014. His sister Kim O'Brien shared, "I miss just about every-thing... His smile, laugh, hugs, advice, all of him." Kim and family, I am sending you all love today and every day.

Kim is just one of the many AFSP volunteers and supporters I've gotten to know over the last few years. She and her family lead the AFSP Out of the Darkness Community Walk team 4Rheal in Central Massa-chusetts each year.

Last year, I was able to walk with Kim for a bit, and it made my heart happy—so often, her social media posts have made me feel seen in my grief and journey as a suicide loss and sibling loss survivor.

*****

May 23, 2024

Today's Healing Miles are in memory of Steve Amirault of Salmon Creek, Humboldt, California, who died by suicide in September 2010. I've remembered Steve many times in the last few years, and I feel him with me on many occasions. I often think he and Teddy would have got-ten along quite well.

His sister Michelle shared, "I miss my big brother beyond measure. He was an amazing self-taught musician, and drums were his passion. I was always in awe when I watched him play; he would tap everything around him when he wasn't playing. We shared a love of music. He was also a kind, compassionate, thoughtful, fair, funny old soul! I can still hear his loud, guttural laugh! He was the best big brother, son, father, uncle, and grandfather. We will always keep his memory alive by sharing our stories and memories and saying his name."

Today is Michelle's birthday, and I saved this day for her as much as for Steve. For surviving siblings, our own birthdays are just as difficult as the birthdays of our lost siblings. They remind us that we continue to grow older while our siblings remain frozen. That longest relationship we should have severed abruptly. Michelle, I am thinking of you and sending you all the love today and every day.

*****

May 28, 2024, on the Isle of Capri, Italy

Today's Healing Miles are in memory of TJ Melton of Portland, Oregon, who died by suicide in April 2019. His mother, Diana, shared, "I miss his goofy, easy-going personality. I miss him calling me mom. I miss everything about him." Sending you so much love, Diana.

While on the Isle of Capri, we walked the hairpin-turn hills against the cliffs of the Krupp estate. It seemed the perfect place to carry Diana and TJ and think about love and loss.

All plants and flowers grew from the limestone cliffs—some scraggly, others lush, but all strong in the face of the strong sea air and barren cliff wall.

It first made me think of that word I dislike... resilience—because it's true. So many of us continue after the loss of our loved ones because we hang on even amidst the storm that rages around and within us.

But then the plants, particularly the pretty purple campanula, reminded me of the hope we find even when things are at their darkest. That was the community I saw in other loss survivors and organizations like AFSP.

I hope you can find that spark of hope when you need it.

*****

May 31, 2024, from Florence, Italy

I intended to walk only a short distance this evening but walked just about three miles after getting turned around in the labyrinth of Florentine streets.

Today's Healing Miles are for Jamie Hunter Boone of Urbana, Illinois, who died by suicide one year ago today. Thinking of his mom, Anita, his whole family, and all who love Jamie.

Anita shared, "I miss hearing Jamie's voice and his big smile that lit up a room when he walked through the door. He was smart, friendly, and had a great sense of humor. I miss him more than life itself."

Anita, I hope you can feel my love across the miles.

*****

September 14, 2024

After yesterday's four-hour long run, I had the gym's treadmills to myself for a seven-mile recovery run.

Today's Healing Miles are in memory of Kent and Deb Weisert, who died by suicide in October 2015 and March 2021, respectively, leaving their daughter Christianna missing her parents and "...Both things that I've lost, and things I never got to experience." She misses her father's wisdom and perspective and her mother's soft-spoken yet powerful voice.

Christianna is one of the many I've met online through my journey—she's one of the many Misfit Runners who've accepted me as I am... but also called me on my bullshit when needed. Christianna introduced me to the concept of SADATURBATING (which I'm prone to do), introduced me to Nicolina's touching song, "Glitter," and often makes me feel seen and heard when I'm feeling less than.

Christianna, even though this is the world's shittiest club ever, I am grateful to walk this path with genuine souls like you. I am holding you in my heart today and every day.

*****

September 19, 2024

I didn't feel great this morning, so I had to get a run in during my lunch. I only had time for three miles, but it's better than nothing. I'll admit that I'm a little disappointed that my hair came out nice today.

Today's Healing Miles are in memory of Ryan Johnson of Palm Harbor, Florida, who died by suicide in March 2020. Like many I've honored this month, I've walked and run in Ryan's memory. Like all the others, his face is etched on my heart, and I always recognize photos of him that his mom, Michelle Johnson, shares immediately.

Michelle shares that of her son, "Ryan was such an amazing son, brother, and friend. He was a giant teddy bear with a huge heart and a wicked sense of humor. He always had a joke or would do funny things, and his incredible laugh is deeply missed. While school shopping, he would send me pictures of the most ridiculous outfits from the dressing room, or he'd find the most obnoxious pair of shoes in the store and wear them around; we never knew what he'd do next. I miss his tight bear hugs and hearing him say, "I love you, Mom." Although his absence has left a huge hole in our hearts, he left us with amazing memories, and we hold onto those as tightly as we can."

Holding onto those memories becomes a full-time job for many of us who only have those left. We'll never have new photos, so we cling to them and the related memories with a vise grip ... even though in doing so, we feel ourselves burning down from the inside out.

I am holding you and all who love Ryan in my heart.

*****

September 24, 2023

I'm awake and dressed early this morning as my family prepares to attend the AFSP Massachusetts Chapter North Shore Out of the Darkness Community Walk in Newburyport, Massachusetts.

Teddy, we all miss you more than words can adequately describe. Today's Healing Miles are for you, our family, and all who knew and loved you.

For those who don't know, my brother … Teddy Fusco, Jr. of East Boston, Massachusetts, died by suicide on May 5, 2017. Teddy was a beloved son, brother, grandson, nephew, cousin, friend, and everyone's favorite uncle. He was a Massachusetts Department of Conservation and Recreation Park Ranger at the Massachusetts State House for nearly two decades. Many who passed through the halls remember his smile, kindness, and love of jokes and shenanigans.

Our lives will forever be separated into the before and after. We wish to hear your laugh just one more time, but instead, look for winks—like blue jay feathers, songs, and the "Jerk Villa" sign I saw during mile eighteen of the Chicago Marathon (after my Achilles partially ruptured!).

I'm grateful to the suicide loss community and AFSP for bringing me hope even amid this tragedy and showing me a path toward healing.

Love you, moron.

Fuckin' Teddy.

*****

Some of these names and stories have lived in my heart for years. Others are ones I've only recently had the honor of carrying. But every single one matters.

This chapter—this collection of miles and memories—reminds us that grief doesn't fade. It doesn't end when the calendar moves forward or the world stops paying attention.

The people we've lost are not just statistics. They are family members, friends, parents, siblings, and children.

They are missed.

They are remembered.

They are oh so loved.

And as long as I can, I will keep running, walking, and speaking their names because love doesn't disappear when someone dies. It lingers in the stories we tell, in how we honor them, in the steps we take to ensure their lives—and their struggles—are not forgotten.

These miles are theirs.

At the beginning of this book, I told you this was never meant to be a self-help book. I don't have the answers and won't pretend I do.

What I have are stories. Stories of grief, survival, running, tattoos, laughter, and advocacy. Stories of falling apart and piecing myself back together again, not neatly and not perfectly, but in a way that's mine.

If there's one thing I hope you take from these pages, it's that there's no right way to heal. No checklist that makes grief easier. No magic number of miles, therapy sessions, or tattoos that make the loss hurt less.

But there is life after. There's a way forward, even when it feels impossible. And it doesn't have to look like mine.

You don't have to run ridiculous distances. You don't have to turn your pain into a cause. You don't have to make your lost person your whole personality (though if you do, I get it). You do have to keep going; however that looks for you. And if all you can do today is exist, that's enough.

Because in the end, what remains isn't just the loss. It's the love. It's the choice, every day, to keep moving forward, even when you have no idea where the road leads.

ABOUT THE AUTHOR

Jen Hoye is a writer, storyteller, and mental health advocate dedicated to breaking the silence around suicide and mental illness. After she lost her brother Teddy Fusco, Jr., to suicide in 2017, Jen channeled her grief into action and advocacy. She is the former board chair for the Massachusetts Chapter of the American Foundation for Suicide Prevention (AFSP), a storyteller with NAMI Massachusetts, and a frequent speaker on the topics of mental health and suicide. Jen received an Illumination Award from Girls Inc. in 2025 for her advocacy work.

Jen created the #HealingMiles program in 2020 as a way to honor those lost to suicide. Since then, she has completed Healing Miles suicide loss remembrance runs and walks for hundreds of men, women, and children from the U.S. and around the globe. She has represented Team AFSP as a charity runner in races like the Boston, Chicago, and Los Angeles Marathons. An avid but incredibly slow runner, as of June 2025, Jen has completed four marathons, eighteen half marathons, and one forty-mile ultramarathon, and has no plans to stop running anytime soon.

Jen lives in Taunton, Massachusetts, with her family and rescue animals—dogs Penelope, Gus, and Daisy; megachonk cat Luna Lovegood; and a small flock of hens, all named Mary-Grace.

Learn more or request a Healing Miles remembrance:
jenniferhoye.com/miles